TRANSFORMATION THROUGH BODYWORK

TRANSFORMATION THROUGH BODYWORK

USING TOUCH THERAPIES FOR INNER PEACE

DAN MENKIN

BEAR & COMPANY
PUBLISHING
SANTA FE, NEW MEXICO

LIBRARY OF CONGRESS CATALOGING-IN-PUBLICATION DATA

Menkin, Dan. 1944-
    Transformation through bodywork : using touch therapies for inner
peace / Dan Menkin.
        p. cm.
    Includes bibliographical references.
    ISBN 1-879181-34-7
    1. Touch—Therapeutic use. 2. Peace of Mind. 3. Mind and body
therapies. I. Title.
    RC489. T69M46   1996
    615.8′ 52—dc20   96-11552
                                                                            CIP

Text Copyright © 1996 by Dan Menkin

Foreword Copyright © 1995 by Robert N. Calvert

Transformation Through Bodywork is an expanded edition of the author's 1995 self-published book, *Facilitating Inner Peace: Exploring the Integration of Transformation-Oriented Bodywork and Inner-Peace Counseling.*

Bear & Company, Inc,
PO Box 2860
Santa Fe, NM 87504-2860

Cover design: © 1996 by Lightbourne Images
Cover photo: Kwesi Arthur
Interior design and typography: Melinda Belter
Printed in the United States of America by BookCrafters, Inc.

To Robert Calvert,
founder of Massage *magazine, whose encouragement and support over the years has resulted in the writing of this book. His farsighted vision and broad understanding of the emerging fields of massage, bodywork, and even inner peace facilitation continue to inspire and nurture so many who are seeking to expand their contributions as healing arts professionals.*

To Melissa Mower and Karen Menehan,
Massage *magazine editors who have personally coaxed, encouraged, and assisted this writer in the continuing process of producing the articles and columns that form the foundation of this book.*

To Michael Robbins,
who has lovingly and faithfully served the author as mentor, psychotherapist, and professional supervisor. Much of the clarity in this writing is a result of Michael's willingness to read and suggest revisions for each column before it was submitted. Much of the wisdom and warmth is a reflection of his wise, open, and compassionate heart.

And, most especially, to the Source,
the Master Healer living within each heart, whose love, joy, and inspiration are the spring from which flows any wisdom appearing in this book.

PERMISSIONS

Special thanks to Bell Tower, 201 E. 50th St., New York, NY 10022, for permission to reprint the excerpt at the end of chapter 15 from *Grace Unfolding: Psychotherapy in the Spirit of the Tao-te ching,* © 1991 by Gregory J. Johanson and Ronald S. Kurtz. 142 pages, $10, paperback. ISBN: 0-517-88130-6; and to *Massage* magazine for permission to reprint José Micaller's illustration on p. 69.

EXCERPTS

Parts of this book have been published or are scheduled for publication in *Massage* magazine as follows: chapters 1 and 2, March-April 1992; chapter 3, November-December 1992; chapter 4, January-February 1994; chapter 6, July-August 1994; chapter 7, January-February 1995; chapter 8, March-April 1995; chapter 9, May-June 1995; chapter 10, July-August 1995; chapter 12, January-February 1996; chapter 13, November-December 1994; chapter 14, September-October 1995; chapter 15, March-April 1996; chapter 16, May-June 1996; chapter 17, July-August 1996; chapter 18, September-October 1996; chapter 19, November-December 1996; chapter 20, January-February 1997; appendix A, March-April and May-June 1994; appendix B ("Cause, Effect, and Compassion"), September-October 1994.

Most of chapter 11 and sections 2 and 3 of appendix B originally appeared in the newsletter of the Guild of (financially) Accessible Practitioners, *Bridging . . . The G.A.P.* Chapter 5 was adapted from an article originally published in the March 1991 issue of *Connections.* The poem preceding chapter 10, "A Touch," is by the author and has been published in both *Massage* and the *Massage Therapy Journal.*

SPECIAL NOTICE TO THE READER

The thoughts and information in this book are offered to inspire and invite contemplation. They are not meant to suggest that one should practice psychotherapy without appropriate training (and licensing if required by law). This book does not claim to be an authoritative text; it may be useful to practitioners, though, as motivation to seek further professional development, study, and training.

As used in this book, the term *inner peace facilitation* is a generic reference to spiritual and personal support; it does not necessarily imply that the facilitator is a professional. Facilitators are advised to give serious consideration to possible consequences before using these approaches, suggestions, and theories with others. Inner peace facilitation can trigger highly complex and unpredictable psychological mechanisms; caution and professional supervision are highly advised.

The characters and events used to illustrate the principles described in this book are fictional, although they are based upon the actual experiences of the author.

Table of Contents

PART ONE

Integrating Touch Therapies and Inner Peace Counseling

CHAPTER ONE

CHAPTER TWO

CHAPTER THREE

CHAPTER FOUR

APPENDIXES

APPENDIX C

Acknowledgments

The author would like to acknowledge and express his heartfelt appreciation to the following people who helped to make this book a reality: Barbara Hand Clow and Gerry Clow of Bear and Company, whose vision and patience with this author turned his self-published, very-limited-edition book into the beautiful, professionally produced edition you now hold; Barbara Doern Drew, professional editor extraordinaire, who saw the "diamond" in this book and spent untold hours "polishing" it; Sharon Seinen, Mary Grace, Brenda Clark, Jean Wright, Marcia Chertok, Coease Scott, Irene Watson, Elizabeth Roach, Gita Beth Bryant, and Jim Fox, who read all or part of the book and offered valuable suggestions for clarification; Franklyn Menkin, Jr., who provided technical proofreading in the early stages and lots of loving encouragement; Paula Menkin, my mother and dearest "fan," who actually read each chapter as it became available and provided wonderful moral support to continue; and David Menkin, my father, whose ongoing encouragement and faith in his son allowed the publishing process to go forward smoothly. Special thanks is also given to all my clients who over the years have provided me with inexpressible inspiration and from whom I have learned much of what appears in this book.

Keep an open mind,
but don't let your brains fall out.
—*Joan Borysenko*

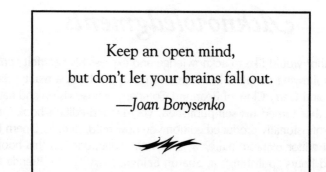

Foreword

Transformation Through Bodywork is a frontline account of the psychological and spiritual situations hands-on practitioners are confronted with in the session room nearly every day. In telling the story of these experiences, Dan Menkin reveals not only the beauty of bodywork, but the opportunities these relationships offer for therapist and client alike. Almost every massage practitioner and bodyworker knows well that the emotional response this work can elicit from clients is something that comes with the territory. Whether seasoned veterans or those just starting out doing relaxation massage, practitioners will encounter the depths of the human predicament in varying degrees of expression at one time or another in their career.

It is because of this universal truth about bodywork that I have encouraged practitioners to write about their experiences in the session room. It is through the shared communication of those who do this work that we first begin openly discussing what all practitioners know. It is from session-room pioneers like Dan Menkin that other less-experienced practitioners can learn what to do when they, too, are faced with emotionally charged situations.

The hairdresser, barber, and bartender listen well, but theirs is a casual meeting place and certainly their interplay is not within the context of a healing relationship. The setting of a full-body massage is obviously more intimate, quiet, and private. Usually the client has little or no clothing on and is being touched just about everywhere—not just on the hair and scalp or just being handed a glass of beer at the bar.

The massage therapist and bodyworker may arguably practice one of the most intimate of professions. In this work clients often express their innermost thoughts and feelings from the depths of their mind *and* physical body. Many in the hands-on healing arts believe that the physical body cannot lie, as the mind can do all too well. The mind and the body are considered one integrated whole in this context, but in more widely accepted terms it is through the body that the mind can be reached and old patterns and feelings can be set free.

It is a combination of the intimate, quiet privacy of the healing relationship and the vulnerability of having one's clothes off and being touched skin to skin that takes the bodywork session into the most private of human realms. But is this psychological realm a place where bodyworkers should venture? Is it an area they can avoid? Are they prepared to deal with these kinds of issues?

Most massage therapists and bodyworkers, in my experience, have little or no formal training in counseling and very little trade education in dealing with the emotional release and intimacy that are often encountered in a bodywork session. There are some courses being offered at schools, but only a limited amount of time is spent on the psychological and spiritual issues related to bodywork—there just is not time in most degree programs only a few hundred hours in length. By and large the massage and bodywork field is poorly prepared in this area.

Most practitioners learn from their own trial-and-error experience within the confines of the session room. To their credit, they help many people despite their lack of training in psychology and counseling. This raises the question about the relationship between being a quality care-giver and having professional training to practice. Most practitioners just want to help others with their pain and suffering.

Dan Menkin shows a sharply perceptive eye toward these types of session-room experiences. He writes directly from his years of experience facilitating a wide range of clientele. He is especially keen on discussing the respective responsibilities of the therapist and client in a bodywork session. The ethics of working on another person's body/mind are significant, and Dan's sensitive and mature approach offers readers much food for thought on this subject of growing concern in the trade.

His observations from the session room are backed up by numerous clinical consultations with an experienced psychotherapist; he has had the advantage of being able to discuss his client interactions with someone who has the training to offer him more perspective and awareness about what is happening than he would have gotten by his observations and reflections alone. This ongoing supervision has been a rare opportunity for Dan and, through his writings, for his readers, too.

Dan's descriptions and gentle wisdom also reveal a changing clientele, a change we find throughout the field. There are more and more people who are seeking optimal health today. They are the new pioneers of the inner self. Although the majority of massage clients seek relief from their pain and stress or come simply just to feel good for a while, there are a growing number of people who are actively seeking the keys to unlocking their barriers to a level of health and well-being beyond just staying fit. These are the people who seek and find a therapist offering facilitation in the transformation of one's total health and being—from simply following a health care plan to recognizing and maintaining a successful personal health process within one's favored lifestyle.

In *Transformation Through Bodywork* we are privileged to encounter the personal transformative process of various clients as they have been facilitated by the author. But the real joy is in knowing that the transformative process is not just for the inner-self pioneers; it is a process available to everyone—that is, anyone willing to acknowledge there is a journey of transformation available to us. More importantly, this book can be a transformative process for the therapist. It provides insight into the language of pain and healing, how the exercise of patience is true compassion, and how the possession and apt use of a considerable repertoire of skills is necessary to be a true professional.

The beauty is that in the end practitioners do not really have to deal with every situation if they know when to say "no" and refer their clients to more suitable professionals. In those cases where this is not necessary, *Transformation Through Bodywork* will help them to be with the person on the table more easily without having a lot of anxiety about what to do next. In many cases listening is enough. But if you don't know that simple fact, you may find yourself struggling despite your best efforts.

Just as the transformative process espoused in this book reveals opportunities for the client's inner peace, so does it present the practitioner with insights and suggestions for creating a safer haven in the session room. Knowing how to respond—and not react—to an emotional release from the client without feeling as if you have to be a psychotherapist goes a long way toward being a safer practitioner.

It is important to realize that this material is not meant to be used as training in how to deal with the psychological and spiritual issues arising from bodywork and massage. Instead it is intended to be used as an information resource, a beginning place from which to further explore the psychological and spiritual ramifications of hands-on therapies. Neither are my remarks meant to encourage the experimental approach to learning how to deal with emotional release from a client. Practitioners should learn first about their personal boundaries and their scope of practice. Then they can learn about the boundaries of others and the interactive process with clients in the session room each day. This book is an interesting and sometimes fascinating look into the therapeutic session room during the transformative process. It can be a guide to practitioners to further study about their clients, themselves, and the interplay between the two in the session room.

I think the popularity of learning more about the psychological factors present in the bodywork session means that practitioners are smart to realize what they need. It may be a sign that a certain level of maturation has been reached in the trade. It is certainly an acknowledgment that a professional response to a client's emotional release in the session room is not only desirable, but is actually necessary in order to raise our profession, as well as our clients, to a higher level of functioning.

Robert N. Calvert
Spokane, Washington
February 1995

Robert N. Calvert is the founder of Massage *magazine.*

Preface

The thoughts in *Transformation Through Bodywork* were originally written as encouragement for bodywork practitioners to include inner peace counseling in their practice, appearing in *Massage* magazine's regular "Facilitating Inner Peace" column from 1993 through 1997. Though much practitioner guidance still remains, this book now offers a much broader invitation for *each of us* to explore our own next steps in personal and professional growth so that we might become more powerful and effective healing environments for ourselves, our relationships, our human family, and our planet.

The major focus of this book is "facilitating inner peace," referring to the support we can provide for ourselves and others in this healing process. As you read, *you* are repeatedly invited to become an *inner peace facilitator*, a person increasingly committed to discovering and melting whatever obstacles block the natural radiance and transforming power of the spirit dwelling within. It doesn't matter whether you are a bodywork professional or an engineer, receive money for your healing work or simply offer what you can "as a friend." The quest to reclaim our birthright of peace and joy is a universal process, and *this process always starts with ourselves.* As our inner light shines more clearly, we become increasingly useful to ourselves and others in the transformative processes now accelerating the evolution of consciousness all over planet Earth.

I welcome hearing from you and learning how these words are supporting your personal quest for inner peace. You can contact me by calling (800) 442-6035.

TRANSFORMATION
THROUGH
BODYWORK
USING TOUCH THERAPIES
FOR INNER PEACE

The greatest revolution of our generation is the discovery that human beings, by changing the inner attitudes of their minds, can change the outer aspects of their lives.

—*William James*

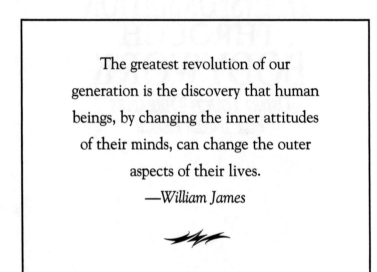

PART ONE

INTEGRATING TOUCH THERAPIES AND INNER PEACE COUNSELING

Faith is the bird that feels the light
and sings when the dawn is still dark.

—*Tagore*

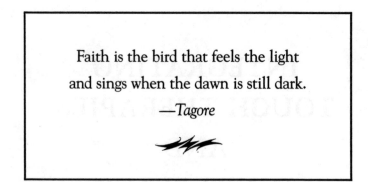

Introduction

There's a new wind blowing—something's changing. Something subtle. Something wonderful! Have you felt it?

In the massage and bodywork professions, many of us have experienced this shift as an increased willingness in clients to explore the roots of their tension—to go beyond the quick-fix mentality and begin to see the old "stuff" inside that causes painful limitation, lack of energy, and a gnawing sense that something is missing in their lives. While they may book a bodywork session because they are tense and perhaps also in pain, a little bit of encouragement will often reveal a much deeper agenda if they but know how to express it. Given a bit of time and skillful support, many are only too eager to explore the possible causes of their complaints.

Increasingly, bodywork clients are seeking the assistance of broad-spectrum somatic educators and healers to better understand chronic constriction in the body as well as in the mental, emotional, and spiritual realms. This exploration eventually uncovers old wounds that, living buried and unhealed inside for decades, breed chronic fear, attachment, and frustrating control patterns.

Of course, these also manifest as chronic muscular constriction, and desire for relief from their discomfort is what brings most people for bodywork in the first place. So if practitioners look with an open, compassionate heart, they will often find opportunities to share their own discoveries for breaking this cycle of tightness.

When an individual has nurtured a certain level of inner peace within, that person naturally becomes a powerful environment for others who are also seeking this peace. Whether practitioner or recipient, the more we follow our own longing to be free of chronic constriction patterns, the more we can offer meaningful, caring, and truly transformative guidance to others. *Transformation Through Bodywork* is designed to enrich and inspire that offering.

Ah, There's the Rub

A Client's Story

The following story is offered to convey the nature of a session combining inner peace facilitation and transformation-oriented bodywork. Although quite abbreviated, I hope this will share a little of the flow, content, and feeling of this work.

"So, Sarah," I say to myself, "is it time to roll over and die?" Every muscle in my body aches, and I wonder, "What's the use? . . ."

But I know better. Even though my car has died, my job stinks, my love life is nonexistent, and I haven't had a decent meditation in weeks, I know I'll go on. I'll face the challenges like I always do, and I'll continue traveling deeper into this tangled forest of my inner self. Today, though, its threatening darkness feels like it's about to gobble me up.

I need help! I need some relief! Thank God I made that appointment for a massage this afternoon!

It's funny how that happened. I was glancing through this magazine and all of a sudden an ad jumped out at me. I started thinking about my aching muscles and chronic tightness. Now, normally massage wouldn't be my cup of tea, but that day I'd had it! Either something changes or . . . Well, maybe some work on the ol' knotted muscles wouldn't be such a bad idea after all. This ad said we'd talk for a while first, which made me feel a little less anxious. And the price was right also.

So here it is, three o'clock, and I just rang the bell—no turning back now! The door opens and butterflies are playing Ping-Pong with my lunch! But Dan, the therapist, seems nice enough, and we go upstairs to a sunny sitting room that's filled with plants and seems . . . really peaceful. He offers me tea, and I choose something soothing. While we're sipping, he explains that the reason the session has been designed to be as long as it is—three hours, no less!—is to give us some time to get to know each other in preparation for the massage.

Before we get into other stuff, though, I have to ask him about his "client- determined fee." Dan smiles and begins to tell me a little about his spiritual beliefs. As he understands it, whatever skills he can offer in the way of massage or counseling come from a higher power. For him it's "God," but he has no attachment to specific words or dogmas. He points to a poster of the blue Earth suspended in the black void of space and talks of his love for her, of the need for each of us to do whatever we can to help humanity wake up and stop hurting her.

So, he says, if through these sessions people relax more deeply and see themselves more clearly, then hopefully they will also discover the will to live more harmoniously with each other and Earth. Since the usual cost for such sessions might be a barrier to some who are otherwise ready to make good use of what this process offers, he has chosen to trust clients to decide their own appropriate fees. Some are quite generous, he says, while others, like myself, may offer something more modest.

When I ask whether he's making out OK financially, he smiles and says yes, that all his needs are provided for. He seems so peaceful and content that it makes me ponder my own chronic anxiety concerning money and my lack thereof. Maybe, I wonder, there are other ways to approach this security thing?

I ask him some questions about his work and he answers, adding that what he most delights in offering is an opportunity for me to learn about my inner self, especially my physical tension patterns, in ways not normally encouraged in daily life. Then, since I look interested, he offers some background information on the history of body-oriented therapy in the West.

Back in the 1930s, Wilhelm Reich developed the idea of chronic muscle tension as a form of internal body armor. This, it turns out, is a clever idea for a defense system created by a child who has no other means of protecting him or herself. Tight muscles block the flow of energy in the body and dull the awareness of pain. According to Reich, mind and body are always reflecting each other, so a blockage of pain in the body also indicates a blockage of awareness somewhere in the mental or emotional realm. Likewise, any mental or emotional conflicts will have their corresponding physical "conflicts," or, as we usually call them, tensions.

The problem, though, is that tightening up in response to fear becomes an unconscious response, a deep habit. As a kid, maybe I did not have other choices, but now, as an adult, this tightening-up habit has become almost like an addiction. It's a disempowering way of relating to life that also consumes huge amounts of energy and leaves me feeling exhausted.

As I'm taking it all in, I can sense how these theories actually describe what I am feeling in my body, what I've been noticing about the way I live my life. It feels good to realize that I'm not alone and that it really *is* possible to discover new ways of responding to frustration and fear. . . .

After about twenty minutes, there's a lull, and Dan's face lights up in a grin as he says, "So tell me, Sarah, why are you here? I don't mean here for this session, but really *here*. Why did you get born? What do you see as the purpose of your life?"

This is not a question I can easily answer, and I confess it is an area where my thinking has been pretty fuzzy. But that doesn't seem to phase him in the least. He keeps feeding me questions that point me to truths deep inside myself that I don't normally pay much attention to. As my ideas begin to form into some sort of pattern, he talks of the importance of "higher vision" in life, of having a sense of what my highest values are so that I can then organize all my lesser values, or desires, harmoniously with these really important ones.

This kind of thinking and exploring is quite challenging and, I have to admit, rather enjoyable. As the time flies by, though, I wonder occasionally what all this has to do with the massage I have come here for. Then suddenly something "clicks" inside and everything falls into place. I can see how all my tangled desires and beliefs are causing this mess of tightness in my body! I want so many things, and when they conflict with each other, I'm "uptight."

I share my insight with Dan, and he agrees. "We could just do a massage here," he says, "and you would feel more relaxed—for a while. But we wouldn't have really solved anything. In fact, we would, in a sense, be continuing an addictive pattern: helpless tension depending on someone else to release it. But by looking inside and seeing how *you* are the cause of your own sufferings, by seeing how *your* mental patterns either empower or disempower your life, well . . . isn't this the road toward greater freedom? Toward a more spacious inner life? Toward real joy?"

As we sit here, delighted and peaceful, Dan gently asks, "When you came in here an hour ago, Sarah, do you remember how you felt? And now . . . do you notice the difference?"

It is true. Even though we have not even begun the massage, my whole body feels lighter, more relaxed. "You see," Dan continues, "when we really focus on the deepest truth inside us, that process itself starts to make us larger in some way. The problems of life don't change, but in relation to the spaciousness of our inner realm, they feel smaller, less problematic."

As we move to the massage part of this session, I am invited to keep these thoughts of my highest vision in mind as I notice the various tensions, aches, and pains that we will be softening and inviting to release. I am shown to a softly lit, warm, deeply peaceful room where I am left alone to get settled. When Dan returns, I am lying on the table, a thick sheet covering me and warm heat lamps recalling memories of sunbathing on a quiet beach. As the next hour and a half unfolds, everything in me settles into deeper and deeper states of relaxation. It is so wonderful to freely enjoy the delightful pleasures arising in my body, knowing that the person drawing them forth will scrupulously observe appropriate boundaries.

Sometimes the work is intense, and Dan invites me to breathe deeply, imagine the tension dissolving, and watch it leave as I exhale. He has encouraged me to say "stop" or "ease up" whenever the work becomes too intense, and a few times I do. But for the most part, the exhilaration of feeling so empowered, so *able* to let go, is worth whatever commitment it takes to process the tension and pain that our work together uncovers.

When my body tour is complete, I am left to bask in the peace and wonder of what I have done over the course of a mere three hours. When I finally choose to get up and slowly amble back to the sitting room, Dan is there smiling, sharing with me the knowledge of the transformation that has just taken place. He said earlier that sometimes people need to talk about what they have experienced and that this time afterward is available for that. But at the moment, I feel so peaceful, so complete, that all I want is to take a solitary walk down the tree-lined street, listening reverently as my heart sings its song of praise to the joy and beauty that pervade all life.

During the following week, I pay a lot more attention to my breathing. In tense situations, thoughts of empowerment and my highest vision surprisingly pop into my head, with their friendly suggestions of alternative approaches to life's seemingly no-win dilemmas. I know now that I am a much more powerful person than I have assumed before, and I am finding all sorts of new and challenging opportunities presenting themselves for my consideration. I know that within me—and especially within this physical self—there exists a universe of truth to be discovered. And it is this unfolding wisdom growing in me day by day that gives hope as I seek to be a more powerful influence for change at all levels of this life we share together.

We must be the change
we wish to see in the world.
—*Mahatma Gandhi*

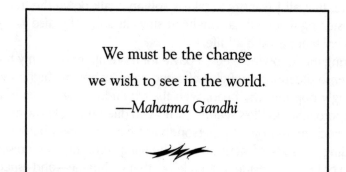

About Transformation-Oriented Bodywork

Highest Vision Confronts Life's "Pain in the Neck"

Among the many forms of touch therapy, psychotherapy, energetic balancing, and spiritual counseling currently available, there is an emerging synthesis of physical, emotional, mental, and spiritual processes that many refer to as "transformation-oriented bodywork" or "transformational bodywork." This is not a modality itself, but rather an *orientation* that can be shared through a variety of different modalities. Its approaches are as varied as the practitioners who offer it, but most share certain fundamental physical and spiritual concepts.

Body Armoring

Wilhelm Reich, an ex-colleague of Sigmund Freud, was one of the first Western researchers to develop the idea that chronic muscle tension is a form of internal body armor. In childhood, Reich pointed out, tightening muscles may have been a person's only available defense against the terror of overwhelming physical and/or emotional pain. Such constricted muscles block the flow of energy in the body, dull the awareness of pain, and give the sense of somehow being solid enough to "take it" and not be destroyed. When this response is utilized by a child over and over again, though, the muscles tend to retain their constriction at deeper and deeper levels, becoming chronically tight and acting as a kind of armor that seems to keep danger out, but also keeps

13

"me" locked in. Over the years, this constrictive response pattern becomes something of an addiction, a disempowering way of relating to life that also consumes huge amounts of energy and leaves one feeling exhausted.

Another pattern that Reich discovered is that mind and body are always reflecting each other. Thus, a blockage of pain in the body also signifies a blockage of awareness—of the memory of the experience that caused the pain originally—somewhere in the mental and emotional realms. Likewise, any mental or emotional conflicts will have their corresponding physical tensions. To describe these patterns of constriction, Reich used the term *character armor.*

Constriction Against Pain

Constriction exists in every realm of our existence. At the spiritual level, it shows up as pettiness, as having a vision of life that lacks expansiveness. On the heart level, we "close our hearts" and pretend, "I don't need anybody!" On the mental level, there are thought patterns that were appropriate for childhood, but that are now much too limited for the adult options available. And physically, there's chronic tension, being "uptight," and the internalizing of others who are a "pain in the neck."

All of these habits of constriction are to some degree an effort to defend against the consciousness of pain. There's the spiritual pain of feeling distant from God or one's inner truth, the emotional pain of fearing of rejection and closing one's heart to love, the mental pain of discovering that a cherished self-image is an illusion, and the physical pain of being hurt. Just as psychotherapy seeks to uncover the hidden mental and emotional pain and evolve more freeing ways of dealing with it, so does transformational bodywork offer an opportunity to discover and change lifelong habits of muscular contraction.

Transformation-Oriented Bodywork

Evolving out of the disciplines of Reichian therapy, bioenergetic analysis, massage, and the personal/spiritual–growth movement, transformational bodywork is shaped by each practitioner's unique combination of skill and experience. Some bring to their practice advanced academic degrees and certification from nationally recognized professional associations. Other practitioners have developed their skills from self-guided education, sharing not as "experts," but as co-seekers in a quest for greater wisdom and peace.

The formats offered for this work are also varied. Many practitioners utilize the common one-hour session, have fixed fee structures, work in clinics or professional offices, and maintain the "professional detachment" often found in psychotherapy and some forms of massage. Other practitioners are experimenting with longer sessions, self-determined fee structures, working in more informal, comprehensively designed environments, and developing interactive styles that emphasize what is shared in the process of personal unfolding and downplay the practitioner as an "authority." Regardless of how their practices are structured, however, ethical bodywork practitioners share a commitment to maintaining clear boundaries as they pursue the work of freeing physical, emotional, and mental energy, being careful to avoid subtle or overt exploitation of sexual energy in their professional relationships.

Empowerment Through Breathing

One major element in this work is education about breathing patterns and their relationship to empowerment. During a bodywork session, as the work goes deeper there is a tendency to reenact old constriction-against-pain patterns both by tightening various muscles and by "tightening up" the breath. As physical discomfort and its accompanying emotional energy become more intense, many recipients breathe more shallowly or, as often happens, end up ceasing to breathe at all for a while. Noticing this, the practitioner might suggest a deep, slow, rhythmic breathing pattern as an alternative approach.

As the breath deepens, the recipient may notice that much of the anxiety-related muscle holding diminishes. Understanding this cause-effect relationship between breathing patterns and overall body tension can be used to one's advantage in a wide variety of life situations.

Another empowering tool utilizes a simple visualization exercise. While continuing deep, full, rhythmic breathing physically, the recipient is invited to imagine that each breath is also an inhalation of healing light directed to the muscle area being massaged at the moment. The muscle's tensions and pains are then imagined to be something dark (like coal dust) that the breath dissolves during inhalation and then is exhaled outward to a nearby candle flame. There it is burned into pure healing light that is once more inhaled, continuing this process of "spiritual recycling."

These approaches to transformational bodywork have much in common with the inner work of hatha yoga (see chapter 17). In a yoga *asana*, the posture assumed generally uses gravity to impose stretching on a specific muscle group. The essence of the yoga practice, though, involves using the breath and the will to relax and release more deeply with each exhalation. In transformational bodywork, it is the practitioner's hands that introduce the stretch. The inner work of the recipient is the same.

The transformational bodywork session, then, acts as a laboratory for deepening self-empowerment skills. These evolve in part out of consciously working with breath and using it to bring more awareness to physical, mental, emotional, and spiritual pain while developing the ability to "let go" on each level more fully.

The Spiritual Warrior

As one becomes more competent in confronting, processing, and releasing the hidden causes of constriction, an uplifting sense of personal power emerges. A useful term for describing one committed to using this power for greater freedom in all realms is "spiritual warrior."

For any warrior, two characteristics are essential. The first is service to a high ideal. Commonly that is seen as the nation. Today, though, many are coming to realize that no ideal smaller than the planetary level will suffice to deal with the "battles" that currently face humanity.

The Highest Ideal

The "highest ideal" or vision lies in the realm of the Divine, from which both we and our planet derive our life and meaning. To see oneself as a spiritual warrior, then, is to see one's focus or purpose in life as service to this ultimate source. For some, the Divine, also referred to as the Source, is understood in terms of one or more of its transcendent qualities, which might be termed Love, Truth, Peace, Freedom, and Joy.

A powerful aspect of transformational bodywork comes from encouraging and supporting each recipient in the process of clarifying and articulating her or his own highest ideal. As practitioners become more skillful in separating personal beliefs from their professional role as client-centered facilitators, it becomes easier to "feel" recipients' reality systems and assist them nonjudgmentally in developing a clear articulation of their own highest vision. This shared understanding can then be incorporated into a focusing statement, or dedication, at the beginning of the bodywork session. It is also useful in supporting the recipient during the session should the fear and anger emerging from the musculature seem to become overwhelming. Simply reminding, "Remember your vision, remember why you are doing this," at an appropriate moment can draw forth tremendous reserves of courage.

Skillful Means

The second essential characteristic of the warrior is the use of "skillful means." For instance, if one sees one's high ideal as the military defense of the nation, then the warrior's skillful means would lie in the realm of martial arts. When, however, one focuses on serving one's source, or the Divine, then skills of a different nature might be called for.

If one imagines Divinity as a focal point of Love, Peace, Freedom, Truth, and Joy, and if one further believes that this "point" is alive and accessible inside oneself, then perhaps the simplest and most direct way to serve this highest ideal is to allow it to emerge freely, unfettered by the personality's limited likes and dislikes. Many have yearned at times, "Lord, thy will be done!" Yet when a life is honestly observed, without the filters of personal bias, it is usually discovered that the limited personality, and not the deepest spirit, is in the driver's seat. So in this context, skillful means refers to the ability to realize—to make real—a life in harmony with one's highest truth.

As it turns out, this ability lies not in acquiring more and better "stuff," whether possessions or experiences. Rather, it is actualized by letting go of old "stuff"—habits, thoughts, and feelings—that constricts one's identity into something much too small for the ideal the spirit within yearns to serve.

Constriction and the Spiritual Warrior

One way, then, of defining the skillful means required of a spiritual warrior focuses on the process of discovering and transforming old patterns of contracting against what is feared. Utilizing a wide variety of resources, the spiritual warrior confronts chronic armoring in whatever form it appears, challenging it to yield its rigidity and evolve into a dynamic, intelligent ally in a whole, integrated life permeated with freedom.

Within this general understanding of skillful means, there are specific attributes to be developed by both practitioners and recipients. Not all who come for transformational bodywork are clear about what this process entails. Therefore, a significant part of the initial interview involves drawing out the aspiring spiritual warrior in the recipient and ascertaining its relative strength as opposed to the recipient's inner resistance and tendency to cling to old patterns.

Recipient Qualities

In appraising readiness for the deeper focus of transformational bodywork, there are two qualities or experiences in a recipient that are most important. The first is having experienced a "glimpse" of the reality hinted at by one's highest vision. From this memory, renewed commitment can be drawn forth again and again as the inner world of blockage and fear is explored. Not surprisingly, many who are drawn to transformational bodywork have experienced some sort of life-changing transcendental "glimpse," though it may take a bit of probing and encouraging from the practitioner to bring it out and shape it into a clear statement of "That's It! That's what I want as the focus of my life!"

The motivation that this "glimpse" provides might alternatively be present in its negative form—an experience or growing awareness that reveals the unmanageability of one's life as it is currently being lived. Very often this realization has led to joining a twelve-step program or seeking some form of counseling. As one matures into one's "sobriety," it may become appropriate to tackle limiting tendencies through bodywork also. Many from this background bring a strong vision (or perhaps an intense desire to avoid falling back into old dysfunctional behavior) that can be drawn forth to support the work.

The second important recipient quality is a willingness to confront, or at least experience, inner pain within the context of growing into greater freedom. While stretching constricted muscles is the *apparent* source of this pain, with skilled guidance the recipient soon learns that the real cause is the fear of "seeing" what the constriction is blocking. As the recipient becomes more adept at interpreting the jumbled experience of pain, she or he learns to discriminate between the sensation of simple physical pain (which most can deal with fairly well) and the subtler commingled emotional pain (with its patterns of resistance and denial) stemming from the unfinished experience of earlier trauma. Often, with appropriate coaching from the practitioner, a recipient is able to draw forth from within a level of courage and focused attention that allows relaxing into and releasing deeper levels of pain than previously had been thought possible.

In connection with this process of confronting and releasing buried emotional pain, it is essential that the recipient have available additional support should the feelings or memories released prove to be unexpectedly intense or confusing. The energy and memories released in this kind of intense bodywork session can often continue to unfold over a period of several days or even weeks. Therefore, it is advantageous for the recipient to be currently working with a psychotherapist or some other type of counselor capable of offering further support and processing after the bodywork session.

(Please note that this "confrontational" approach is only one of many effective orientations to transformational bodywork. Other styles avoid stirring up "old stuff" and focus instead on movement reeducation, gentle "let go" bodywork, or "energy healing," to name a few. Hopefully, the approach chosen will reflect both the practitioner's field of competence *and* an insightful appraisal of the recipient's needs and abilities.)

Practitioner Qualities

For one who would skillfully guide a transformational bodywork session, there are several additional qualities that are quite necessary. Some of these include:

❖ A well-developed ability to enter into a recipient's inner world—to "feel" what is being experienced on the other side of the practitioner's healing hands so clearly that it is possible to "surf the pain." This means sensing the maximum amount of pressure a muscle can endure without tightening against the pain and then staying just below this threshold as the stroke progresses at a snail's pace along the muscle's length. This requires being able to "hover" for minutes on end, skillfully maintaining a loving yet confrontational prespasm pressure.

It also means remaining open to a recipient who is experiencing fear and pain that has been hidden inside for decades. This is not easy! It is a skill, though, that offers the recipient an invaluable opportunity to experience and release very deep levels of constriction and also the corresponding sense of joy and freedom that so often accompanies this release.

❖ Remaining creatively alert to what is happening in the moment (as opposed to applying a preconceived theory or process that may not be appropriate).

❖ A willingness and ability to remain in the presence of sometimes intense discomfort. This can occur physically in oneself as a very long, deep, slow stroke is applied. Discomfort can also arise empathetically in facilitators who are "being with" the emerging pain of the recipient and allying their will with the recipient's process of release and "letting go." In order to do this, it is sometimes necessary to move beyond the desire of a healer to "fix it" comfortably (perhaps ending the releasing process prematurely) and instead listen intensely for what this moment's unique warrior-training process calls for.

❖ Taking time to appropriately cleanse and refresh oneself between sessions. While deeply rewarding, this type of bodywork is often quite draining. If there is not sufficient time for renewal between sessions, both the practitioner and upcoming recipients can suffer.

❖ An awareness of the limits of one's professional skills and sufficient humility not to claim or imply abilities beyond those limits. The nature of this work shares many of the dangers inherent in psychotherapy, yet few practitioners have had the training necessary to recognize and successfully navigate them (see appendix A). One of the primary dictates of a healing arts professional is "Do no harm," and so one aspect of a practitioner's skillful means is choosing to err on the side of restraint rather than get caught up colluding in a "go for it" mentality that ends up going too far.

Some basic understanding of the psychological principles of "transference" and "countertransference" in the practitioner-recipient relationship is most important. (Workshops and classes are sometimes available through body-oriented and body-centered psychotherapy training institutes, universities, community colleges, etc.) It is vital to remember how easy it is to get in over our heads and, even with the best of intentions, inadvertently release memories and emotions that neither the recipient nor the practitioner is capable of handling. This is especially true when dealing with survivors of sexual abuse/incest, where denial may mask the severity of the emotions until "all hell breaks loose." (For additional information on transference and countertransference, see appendix A.)

In short, the most important quality needed is the practitioner's own devotion to becoming a skilled spiritual warrior. From this position of awe and humility before one's own highest vision, there is great fertility from which one may possibly midwife the emergence of another's Joy.

Our Blue Planet

As the aspiring spiritual warrior follows the call to evolve beyond the level of common tensions and limitations, a new life of deepening understanding and heightened ability to love and serve unfolds. Working together, recipient and practitioner are often united in a desire to use these unfolding abilities for the benefit of all humanity and for the healing of our planet.

In a common example, the recipient is employed in a high-stress job working to improve conditions for the poor, the disenfranchised, or the environment. As energy that had previously been tied up in inner conflict and constriction patterns becomes released and available for other uses, recipients often report renewed enthusiasm for their work, a heightened ability to "float" over stressful situations that used to cause them to "sink," and an increased joyfulness that infects co-workers and ripples out to enhance hundreds of daily interactions. The sharpening focus on their highest vision and their spiritual warrior's maturing skillful means begins to permeate all aspects of life, making it possible to offer oneself more potently in the service of the Source and of this precious blue planet we call home.

Let's not only think peace,
but let's show people what peace
would feel like if they had it.
—*Deane Juhan*

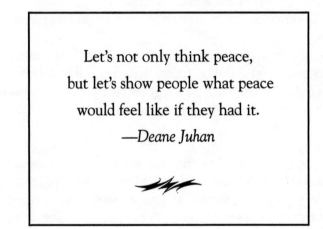

Integrating Inner Peace Facilitation and Bodywork

Several underlying principles guide the processes discussed in this book. The first is that body, mind, and emotions are understood to reflect each other—that treating the body simultaneously affects the other realms and that chronic bodily tension is intimately connected with ingrained mental and emotional habit patterns. This orientation was developed by Wilhelm Reich in the 1930s and 1940s, and expanded upon by Alexander Lowen and the discipline of bioenergetic analysis, among others.

Another principle reflects the simple spiritual idea of a higher power, the Source, from which our abilities as healers (and even inspired educators) flow. These principles are interrelated and become vitally important as we consider the genesis of tension, both in ourselves and in those we seek to serve through bodywork and inner peace facilitation. Exploring this interrelationship begins with a deeper look at the spiritual dimensions of what we offer.

Expansion and Contraction

If we stop to think about it, almost any situation we deal with can be reframed (seen from a different point of view) using the idea of expansion or contraction. For instance, mental-emotional states such as peace, love, and joy are expansive; these feelings and "expanded" consciousness just naturally go together. Likewise, states such as fear, depression, and anger are contractive.

Even our language reveals these truths. After a particularly peaceful or joyful day, we might say, "I feel so up today!" Here, *up* means expansion-ward; the caged spirit feels free to soar joyously through boundless space. And when trouble after trouble comes, we feel "weighed down." Here, *down* refers to a contraction or restriction of the life force in us; our spirit feels constricted to a cramped cage.

We know that constrictive emotional and mental patterns can often become habitual, can seem to take over and lock up most of that naturally free inner space through which our spirits yearn to fly. Likewise, our musculature becomes chronically contracted, never fully letting go, always "on alert." We refer to these inner states in a variety of ways. "I feel so sluggish today" or "My get-up-and-go got up and went" may actually describe not so much an absolute lack of energy as an inner conflict that is binding up (constricting) and consuming most of our energy.

A Driving Illustration

To illustrate, let us suppose that you are a nervous, terrified driver and always inch forward with one foot heavy on the gas and one foot heavy on the brake. Your car is constantly filled with the sickening fumes of burned-out brake linings, you are getting about half a mile to the gallon, and your brakes wear out every hundred miles. You grumble and curse, "They don't make cars like they used to," all the while painfully ignorant of the role your driving habits are playing in this unsatisfactory arrangement.

Now let us say a friend is in the car with you and points out that things would be much easier if you didn't use the brake at the same time you had your foot on the gas. She or he explains how it is your fears—not the car itself—that are making your driving so inefficient. And let us say you "get it" and resolve to change your driving habits. In a burst of enthusiasm, you force your left foot off the brake pedal and . . . instantly you fly forward with a jolt that almost kills you both! After you reassert your brake foot's domination over the car, your friend explains that even though your intentions were wonderful, there are perhaps more appropriate ways to ease yourself into your new, more expansive driving habits.

So together you somehow get to a huge, empty parking lot early one morning, and with tremendous compassion, skill, and patience your friend shows you different, less-constrictive ways to drive. Over and over you experience horrible fears of being out of control, but in the end they melt under the warmth of your friend's loving guidance.

Then one day, after many practice sessions, you find yourself cruising along the open highway, finally experiencing the car the way it was designed to operate. *Say . . .* you think, *not bad!* Your legs are riding lightly on the pedals, skillfully communicating your wishes to the car. You have learned how to handle your conflicting desires inside, no longer imposing them destructively on your vehicle. And you notice that your vehicle "feels" happy, has so much more zip! Hmm . . .

Often bodywork practitioners efficiently "change the brake linings," leaving clients temporarily more functional. But recipients may still be operating at only a tiny fraction of their potential. So perhaps practitioners might consider the role of the "friend" in this story as an inspiration to develop their own abilities as somatic educators and inner peace facilitators. The vehicle, of course, is our body, eager and well-designed to serve us. But it requires that we understand its nature and not overwhelm it with impossible demands. Because of our habitual fear, though, we've lost our innate peaceful relationship with our physical self. We "drive" it, but mostly refuse to accept "it" as "me." We tend to deny the obvious fact that "its" pain is *my* pain, that using "it" abusively is the cause of "my" suffering.

Inner Peace Facilitator as Spiritual Friend

We hunger for a "friend" who will encourage us to go inward and provide a safe and supportive environment for perceiving and dealing with the multitude of conflicting demands we discover there. But who will help us? Who will be there as we timidly attempt to own and rearrange these ancient patterns of inner conflict? Who will "touch" us with such caring, with such skilled compassion, that we feel more confident and empowered to do what needs to be done? Whether it be a social friend or a compassionate practitioner, one thing is sure: this guide will be someone who has "been there," who knows at least some of "the way" from his or her own inner explorations. It will be someone whose heart, having found the grace to receive, now yearns to share its blessing by giving.

Remember, even though most practitioners begin their careers offering temporary symptomatic relief, they can at any time choose to redefine their service more broadly. The same clients who arrive seeking escape from something negative also harbor some degree of hunger for the positive experiences of peace, freedom, and living in joyous harmony with their bodies. As practitioners provide the "relief"—the bodywork their clients seek—they can also share whatever they have to offer as inner peace facilitators. As openings emerge, clients can be helped to reframe their current difficulties in terms of expansion and contraction and can be supported in exploring options that nurture the expansion for which their hearts long. Each of us can demonstrate through our lives—through the spacious offerings of our joyful hearts—that expansion of body, mind, heart, and spirit leads to Truth. "And the Truth shall set you free."

"But What Do I Do?"

This all sounds well and good, you may be thinking, *but what do I say? What do I do as an inner peace facilitator?* There are, of course, books to read, workshops and seminars to take, practices to follow; these are important and definitely have their place. In later chapters we will discuss several useful approaches.

Along with these, you can follow two simple guidelines. One is to remember those supports that have been useful to you in pursuing your own inner peace and offer these as gifts to those you serve. A sense of safety, a tranquil environment, help in clarifying the confused strands of inner vision, help in reframing current problems that allows your own unique solutions to emerge—whatever touched and supported *you* in situations similar to ones you are now facing can also be of assistance to others.

The second guideline is to *remember.* Remember to maintain your own inner peace *no matter what.* Your peace and wisdom are integral parts of your inner being, but most of us keep loosing track of them— forgetting. So we "re-member": we draw back the separated peace-member of our inner family of self. When we are solid in this place of calm, we often hear the "still, small voice within" suggesting just the right thought to share, showing us when to be silent, when to speak. From that place of stillness inside, healing hands find their inspiration, thoughts their guidance. When we work from that place, joy and compassion emerge; they are contagious.

Al's Story

The story of Al offers a brief example how inner peace facilitation and bodywork can be joyfully integrated. Al worked as a store clerk doing heavy menial labor, was in his late thirties, had grown tremendously from various twelve-step programs, and was at the time enrolled in college seeking a master's degree in counseling. His initial motivation for massage was physical: his body ached. As we worked together, though, it became clear that Al "ached" at a deeper level also. He longed to be free of the humiliating situation in which he earned his living; he yearned to have all his time and energy available to study for his career-to-be. And his inner turmoil, his resistance to accepting things the way they were at that time, was consuming precious energy he couldn't spare.

Observing this, I encouraged Al to talk before and during the bodywork, to give voice to the suffering he was "embodying." The bodywork began to follow the rhythm of his mental and emotional releasing. He responded nicely to suggestions to breathe, to notice what he was feeling in certain areas, to observe how letting go of certain ideas allowed the bodywork to move deeper, to release bound-up energy, to access inner peace.

While I had no ability to cancel the negative effects of forty hours a week of grueling labor, I *could* provide Al with a place for releasing its toxic by-products, for reframing its meaning, and for focusing more deeply on the larger picture that gave him the patience and energy to endure. In addition to bringing relaxation to his body, Al's sessions also brought peace and joy to his mind. Along with feeling "touched" through his skin and muscles, Al left feeling that his hidden inner beauty had been heard, seen, appreciated, and nurtured.

So the bottom line is this: administering short-term fixes uses only a small part of our healing potential. Educating ourselves in the art of inner peace—and sharing what we're learning with others—facilitates expansion of consciousness, increased ability to deal creatively with life's stresses, and long-term transformation. In these days of intense change, of forces everywhere pushing us into uncharted waters, can we as conscientious human beings offer each other anything less?

To get on with our life means looking at
some of the stuff we've been struggling
our whole life not to see. Grace is not
always pleasant, but it always brings us
closer to our true nature.

—*Stephen Levine*

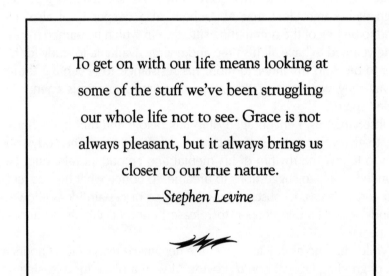

Spirituality:
A Path Toward Inner Peace

Jung spoke of the archetype called the wounded healer. I believe that each wound we suffer and eventually heal from is a soul-making experience with the potential to awaken our willingness to participate in the healing of our world.

We are living in an unprecedented time. The world soul is truly on fire with hunger, pollution, and hatred. Many of us are wounded. And it is up to each person to use the fire of their wounds consciously—to heal, to work for peace, to transform our world. If we do not, the fire in our souls will burn us up both individually and collectively. Our cities will burn, our children will turn to drugs, our earth will become too polluted to sustain life. More and more people—paradoxically through pain, abuse, and trauma—are literally seeing the light and committing themselves to personal and societal healing.

To be healers we need to go beyond being victims or even survivors of whatever our own private hell might be. We are being called upon instead to become transformers of consciousness.

—*Joan Borysenko,* Fire in the Soul

Technician or Healer?

Painful though it may be, many bodywork practitioners are finding themselves confronted repeatedly in their work with some fundamental questions: Am I merely a well-trained technician objectively applying my technical training, or do I accept the responsibilities of being a healer [as suggested in the quote above] within whatever boundaries are appropriate for my personal experience and evolution, offering *myself* as an environment for clients to heal in *if they choose?*

If our goal is the second option, sooner or later we need to deal with the old truism "You can't give what you don't have." While most of us can offer technical competence and a certain amount of caring, a haunting question still remains: To what degree can I offer *myself* as a living example of dynamic inner peace?

In our world today, the marketplace abounds with healing professionals who embody the very diseases from which their clients seek to be free. There is the medical doctor who smokes, the psychologist who has a drinking problem, the pastoral counselor whose weak boundaries lead him into sexual intimacies with a client, the dietitian who is a junk-food addict. The phenomenon is so common that we hardly bother to feel disgusted any more.

Then one day, in a rare moment of clear vision, we might look into the mirror and see that this bodywork professional—the "expert" sought by our clients in their quest for peace—has, perhaps, a nervous twitch, chronic irritability, raging conflicting desires, unexplored subconscious values giving rise to unwanted habits . . . the list goes on and on. In an honest self-examination, each of us can customize it to our own unique personal situation.

The Law of Resonance

"But, hey," you say, "that's my personal life. As long as what I offer my clients is professionally correct, what difference does it make?" To answer that question, consider the "law" of resonance, which you can easily verify from your own experience: *inner states of being are contagious.* When I am around someone who is joyful, I tend to feel more joyful; when I'm around someone who is distraught, I tend to feel unhappy also. Like twin tuning forks, when one is vibrating the other just naturally tends to vibrate at the same frequency.

So if you truly aspire to provide an environment in which clients can process and let go of inner tension and conflict, the law of resonance suggests that this will be possible only to the degree that you have freed *yourself* from inner conflict. In twelve-step programs this is called "walking your talk." Or put another way, what you *are* speaks more loudly than what you *say*. And trying to cheat by separating the *personal me* from the *professional me* just doesn't work, especially in a hands-on profession where the physical, and hence emotional, link transmits so much of our inner self.

"All right," you say, "I'll buy that what's going on inside me affects my work with my clients. Now what?"

This leads us to the realm of spirituality. Spirituality here does not mean any particular religion or mystical tradition, but rather it is a term referring to the science and practice of seeking profound truth within and, ultimately, the very source of that truth. This source could be called "Spirit," or it could be thought of as our true self, inner guide, higher power, or God within. The terminology is not important here; what matters is that we seek and discover the part of ourselves that knows what's what, that sees things as they really are—that is *living* truth. Then, in the words of the great sages, "the truth shall set you free." Free, that is, from the dis-ease within. Free from feeling separated from your innate inner harmony. Free to be the radiant, loving person you truly are. And free to be a powerful healing environment for clients seeking this same freedom in themselves.

Healing Versus Curing

Perhaps here it is appropriate to differentiate between what is meant by *healing* and what is more commonly sought, which could be called *curing*. Curing refers to the removal of an undesired symptom. For instance, when I take an aspirin to reduce the pain of a headache, I may be curing the symptom called "headache," but I am doing nothing to affect the underlying *cause* of my "dis-ease." The word *disease* is intentionally divided here to remind us that painful symptoms are usually warnings that something is out of balance within—that somehow we have lost our natural "ease" in living. Turning off this warning message may only set the stage for our inner physician to seek our cooperation with ever more attention-getting symptoms.

Healing, in contrast to curing, is an act of will, even if that act is only to cease resisting, let go, and allow healing energy to enter and perform its work inside. In other words, healing requires conscious cooperation. The traditional advice "God helps those who help themselves" seems reflective of this truth, although discovering *how* to help ourselves while staying in tune with Spirit is easily a lifelong process. So while curing can happen *to* you, healing must in some way be invited and accepted *by* you.

One often overlooked truth is that sometimes healing does *not* include the removing of troublesome symptoms. But it always includes the expansion of acceptance and inner peace. For a rich and deeply compassionate exploration of this topic, see *Healing into Life and Death* by Stephen Levine.

Bodywork practitioners are constantly being pulled between demands to cure clients and the requirements inherent in genuine, lasting healing. Curing is relatively quick, doesn't rock the boat, and leaves everyone feeling good for the time being. Healing, on the other hand, generally takes much more time and effort, often requires looking at parts of ourselves that we chronically deny, and may in its earlier stages actually intensify feelings of dis-ease before resolution occurs.

This is really one of the core questions humanity faces at this time: Do we do what's easy in the short term, get quick symptomatic results, and leave the underlying problems to fester and grow? Or do we "bite the bullet," acknowledge that we have lost something precious, and seriously do whatever it takes to regain our natural individual and collective "ease" or harmony? Practitioners may feel there is very little they can personally do to change the world, but there is tremendous possibility of healing ourselves and then, through the law of resonance, being powerful healing environments for others.

Truth and Healing

So genuine healing means accepting things inside and out *as they really are*. It means harmonizing one's thoughts, words, and actions with the highest truth one can perceive. And in times of inner conflict, when two or more "truths" present themselves and pull us in opposing directions, it means courageous application of the spiritual law that says, "The lesser shall give way to the greater."

This highest truth can be thought of as Spirit, as God, as one's higher power. So the healing process seeks Spirit as an inner mirror to reveal those patterns hidden inside that disrupt our natural peace. If one is comfortable calling this mirror God, then prayer is an excellent means of accessing its wisdom—of opening one's heart in readiness to receive its truthful reflection. If one prefers to think of the ultimate source in less personal terms, then instead of prayer there might be inner dialogue with the higher self, meditation to access inner stillness (see clearly what is in the mirror), and a whole host of other spiritual practices proven over millennia to expand the consciousness of the sincere seeker. In short, the technique is much less important than the intensity and purity of the seeker's motivation.

As I honestly seek my own inner healing by accessing and following the guidance of my inner spirit, something simple yet profound may happen: my trust of this voice of intuitive wisdom—this inner mirror of truth—grows. Over time I discover that when I follow its lead, things somehow work out just fine. And when I ignore its guidance, even though I may get some pleasure in the short run, somehow over time things do not go as well.

To the degree that I have deepened my attunement and willingness to follow this inner guide in pursuing my own peace, I will naturally have that much more access to its wisdom as I seek to help others. Another way of saying this is that insofar as I have learned how to "get out of my own way," I am able to operate as a channel or conduit for higher healing power to *flow through me* for the benefit of others.

So what I perceive as the *source* of my healing ability has major consequences. If I feel "I" am "doing healing" on my client, then the possibilities are limited to whatever abilities "I" have acquired. If, on the other hand, there is a higher power operating *through* me, then the healing possibilities are limited only by my ability to melt and allow it to shine.

The Meaning of Life

This concept is illustrated beautifully in the following anecdote (author unknown):

"What is the meaning of life?" was asked of Alexander Papaderos, the renowned Greek philosopher.

Taking his wallet out of his hip pocket, he fished into a leather billfold and brought out a very small round mirror, about the size of a quarter. And what he said went like this:

"When I was a small child, during the war, we were very poor and we lived in a remote village. One day, on the road, I found the broken pieces of a mirror. A German motorcycle had been wrecked in that place.

"I tried to find all the pieces and put them together, but it was not possible, so I kept only the largest piece. This one. And by scratching it on a stone I made it round. I began to play with it as a toy and became fascinated by the fact that I could reflect light into dark places where the sun would never shine.

"I kept the little mirror, and as I went about my growing up, I would take it out in idle moments and continue the challenge of the game. As I became a man, I grew to understand that this was not just a child's game but a metaphor for what I might do with my life. I came to understand that I am not the light or the source of light. But light—truth, understanding, knowledge—is there, and it will only shine in many dark places if I reflect it."

In closing this chapter, I would like to share a letter I received from a client and professional colleague:

From often feeling overwhelmed by the enormity of our global situation, I am again reminded that empowering individuals is just as an effective tool for change as more overt forms of activism—maybe even more so! Now there's a concept— massage as activism! Needless to say, my contact with the ideas of transformational bodywork is still rippling change within and hopefully without to the people I work with.

So you see, these are powerful principles we are working with here. May your heart guide you well in discovering your own unique ways of serving and transforming.

It does not matter how long you have forgotten,

only how soon you remember.

—*The Buddha*

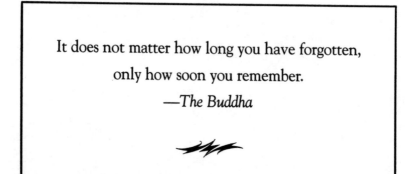

The Thunder of the Floes

Awakening Individual Consciousness
and Planetary Transformation

As we develop our professional skills and continue unfolding our inner wisdom and healing capacity, we might also recall our interconnectedness with what's happening all over the world. Today many of us are feeling deep personal anguish as we listen to the news, as we observe our beloved Mother Earth becoming more and more wounded by our human thoughtlessness, as we hear the tales of suffering and inner turmoil that our friends are sharing. Our own lives, too, are often increasingly confused. Many of us feel as if we are slipping further and further out of control. We may at times feel assaulted by despair, by a longing to somehow make sense of the growing chaos and destruction intensifying around us.

But then there are also those occasional blessed moments when something enters our consciousness, and it all begins to make some sort of sense. It might be an insight from a teacher, a loving word from a friend, or a few inspirational lines such as these from the play *A Sleep of Prisoners* by Christopher Fry:

The human heart can go the lengths of God.
Dark and cold we may be, but this
Is no winter now. The frozen misery
Of centuries breaks, cracks, begins to move,
The thunder is the thunder of the floes,

The thaw, the flood, the upstart Spring.
Thank God our time is now when wrong
Comes up to face us everywhere,
Never to leave us till we take
The longest stride of soul men ever took.
Affairs are now soul size.
The enterprise
Is exploration into God.
Where are you going? It takes
So many thousand years to wake,
But will you wake for pity's sake . . .

And perhaps we wonder, *Could this be true?* Could it be that our shared history as a people has been only a winter's drama on a frozen river? What if after aeons of building ice palaces, we have forgotten that winter is, after all, the season that precedes spring?

The Coming Spring

Those stirrings in our hearts that long for a world of peace, of harmony, of genuine caring and respect for all life—is it possible that these are the harbingers of a coming springtime? If indeed the "thunder" that we hear all around is the "thunder of the floes, the thaw, the flood, the upstart Spring," then the work before us is not quite so overwhelming—we are not required to "make spring happen." Not only would that be absurd, but such thoughts distract us from what we are truly called upon to offer in support of this natural and irresistible process.

If indeed a new springtime of consciousness is unfolding upon this planet, if the changes we are seeing around us are arising out of some kind of grand-scale thaw, a melting of old ways and life structures, then how are we to respond and participate in this emerging season of spiritual light? In many folk cultures, the arrival of spring brings with it mother's "spring tonic," an herbal formula designed to purge the body of toxic wastes accumulated over a long winter. Might then our Mother Earth currently be offering us a "spring tonic," a series of experiences, challenges, and spirit-stretching longings of the heart formulated to purge our souls of the toxic negativity, anger, pettiness, and self-centeredness with which they have become increasingly poisoned?

Melting Ice Structures

It is as if we have been playing in our ice structures on winter's frozen river for so long that we have forgotten that our true home is the solid earth, not this temporarily hardened water. Perhaps the callous, self-centered, cold, and uncaring ways of humanity these past millennia have been a "winter of the spirit." For too long have we huddled shivering in our snow huts on the frozen rivers of our hearts, forgetful that there are other ways to live, other seasons to be longed for.

Now, however, like the winter-bound Northerner suffering from cabin fever, our yearning has been heightened. The slightest scent of approaching spring sets our noses quivering, and we remember warmth, remember green, and intensify our preparations for this season of joy. For those of us ensconced in our ice homes on this frozen but increasingly unstable "river of the world," this means relocating to the shore. While the land is not yet fully remembered by most of us, deep in our hearts we know that it is not so very far away and that it is a place quite safe from the devastation and crumbling reality of our thawing river world.

And what is this "shore," so close and so safe? The Great Ones of all religions have spoken of it as the inner self, the land of "the still, small voice within" that knows what's what—that profound silence within where we truly *see* reality. With this insight, even as we continue to fulfill our commitments in the world, we can also nurture our longing for genuine warmth—we can also do the inner work that moves us closer toward that not-so-far shore where we can feel directly the solid reality of Truth, Love, Peace, Freedom, and Joy.

There are many ways of moving toward one's inner shore. Teachers abound in traditional methods of contemplation, prayer, meditation, and yoga. And the *inner* teacher is always present, whispering the way to ears free enough from the noise of negativity and egotism to hear.

Challenging Mirrors

When our resolve weakens, when doubt begins to blur commitment, the coming spring sends mirrors in many forms, challenging us to see and change those "heavy" habits of the mind that the crumbling ice of our passing winter can no longer support. We may then indeed feel as if "wrong comes up to meet us everywhere." But these perceptions of wrong are also the heralds of a wondrous spring, are the stomachaches that signal Mom's tonic is doing its job.

This inner awareness of our wrong ways, while humbling and often not pleasant, also bears an invitation to take "the longest stride of soul men ever took." As our hearts accept this invitation from the unfolding divine light, from our longed-for future, we are led to bring our personal lives in harmony with the lawful ways, the *dharma*, of this dawning era of truth and harmony for Gaia and her people.

Walking on the crumbling river, overwhelmed with "the thunder of the floes," still we each have choices. If we allow ourselves to become paralyzed with fear, we will eventually drown. But if we can recall in our hearts that memory of springtime's warmth and light, can somehow sustain our vision of the joy, beauty, and rightness that is coming of its own accord, then perhaps we will also find within us the will and power to do whatever is needed to move these tired feet a few more paces toward the waiting shore. And even as our work continues there, tender green shoots will be tickling our feet, and the blooms of the early crocus will bring delight to these winter-weary hearts.

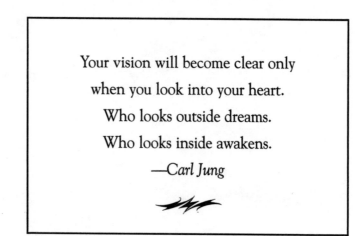

Your vision will become clear only
when you look into your heart.
Who looks outside dreams.
Who looks inside awakens.

—*Carl Jung*

PART TWO

FACILITATING INNER PEACE: CLIENT WORK, PRACTITIONER WORK

That fire of clear mind is in everyone, and to remove any obscuration of its clarity is the duty of all people in this time, that each one may remember and find our way again to the source of our being.

—*Dhyani Ywahoo*

A Client-Practitioner Dialogue

The following is another sample of a prebodywork dialogue incorporating some of the ideas previously discussed. The anecdote is obviously abbreviated and leaves out a tremendous amount of the inner peace facilitation process. It is offered, though, as an example of how insightful dialogue drawing upon spiritual principles can complement transformation-oriented bodywork to support deep, long-term changes in behavior patterns and their accompanying muscular tension.

Welcoming Carol

"Welcome Carol," I say as she enters my office and awkwardly settles into her chair. As a single mom working fifty-plus hours a week and struggling to end the legal mess of a failed marriage, I *know* she's going to be tense. Pain radiates from her face as we engage in small talk, giving her a few moments to adjust to the peace and safety of this environment. Having worked together for seven sessions now, I am aware of her deep longing for inner peace. Carol is a survivor, a deeply courageous person, and someone who is about to go over the edge. Or so it seems to her at this moment.

After a while, Carol pauses, takes a few deep breaths (a process we've shared together often in the past), closes her eyes, and is silent for a minute. Then looking very vulnerable and scared, she turns to me and says, "You know, it's not really my ex or the kids or the job that's driving me crazy—it's something in me. Sometimes I feel I can almost see it, this nagging voice that keeps undermining my self-confidence and throwing me into depression. I hate myself when I can't control that!"

Exploring Carol's Inner Family

My heart aches with Carol's pain and confusion, and I pray that I may be allowed to help her connect with the source of all peace, from which she feels so estranged just now. The bodywork certainly has reminded her what being relaxed and peaceful feels like, but after each session this balanced inner reality seems to vanish before another day has passed. "Why," she has begged, "can't I learn how to retain this inner calmness always?"

As I listen to Carol, I find myself seeing a large family of frustrated children fighting and screaming at each other. Where, I wonder, are the wise elders who might help bring some harmony and direction to this chaos? From our past conversations, I know these wise ones exist in her inner family. But for some reason they have been kept in the background and are rarely invited to bring their wisdom and guidance to her inner conflicts.

So I ask Carol about "Grandmother," her name for the wise woman within. "Grandmother is well," replies Carol, and for a moment a look of wistful longing passes across her face. "What does Grandmother have to say?" I inquire.

Carol closes her eyes, and when she speaks, her voice has a new sense of calm in it. "Grandmother feels so sorry for me," says Carol. "She sees how torn I am by all the different needs and desires pulling at my innards."

"Does she have any advice to offer you just now?" I ask. Carol, who has internalized much of what we have practiced together in previous sessions, nods and says, "Grandmother invites me to be quiet for a few moments and listen for my heart's deepest longing."

Together we sit in silence, my heart yearning for her to find that deep pool of peace and wisdom inside from which she can drink both now and in days to come. At last Carol speaks, and it is clear that she and Grandmother have merged and have begun to comfort and skillfully manage the many cries of need and desire that moments before were propelling her toward madness.

"What I really want is to feel loved, to feel like I belong and don't have to constantly be afraid of being forgotten or hurt. When I become quiet like this, it's much easier to see that there really *is* enough love to go around. But I keep forgetting that and listening to my head's chatter about 'not enough, not enough.'"

"So maybe," I reply, "your head needs some different ways of dealing with its perception of 'not enough.' I don't know if this will help, but here's an interesting metaphor to play with.

A Huge Block of Foam Rubber

"Imagine that in this room there is a huge block of foam rubber," I suggest to Carol. "It is so large that there are just a few feet of space available between its edge and the wall and ceiling. You and I, in an attempt to have more space to work in here, are pushing against this foam rubber with all our might. We are able to compress it and create a bit more room here, but whenever we let go, our hard-won space disappears. So we are constantly pushing, and constantly afraid that our strength will give out and we'll lose everything.

"Now imagine that by accident one day we pause in our Herculean task and rest by leaning against the wall. To our amazement, the wall slides outward and stays there when we stand back. More space! And no fear of losing it. So we turn our attention away from the obstructive foam rubber and instead concentrate all our energy on expanding the walls and ceiling of the room. Gradually it gets larger and larger until it is almost the size of a cathedral. Remembering once more the intrusive foam rubber, we turn around and see that while it has not changed in the least, it is now a nicely proportioned block toward the front on which we can place a lovely cloth and various ornaments. Same block, different building. Same 'problem,' different context."

Carol nods appreciatively, she and Grandmother soaking it in. "All right," says Carol, "I understand that the way I try to focus and push on my problems with my mind is like pushing on the foam rubber. But how do I turn around and work on expanding the walls instead?"

Why Were You Born?

"Why were you born?" I ask, seeming not to pay any attention to her question. "Were you just the biological result of a night of passion, or was some part of you existing before conception, yearning for a human body in which to have certain experiences and learn certain lessons?"

Carol is thoughtful, and I notice that the energy in the room changes subtly. "No," she replies, "I don't believe I was just an accident. I've often thought that I had some existence before this life and that I came here to do something. But I can't remember what."

"Ah, yes. That's a problem so many of us have." Opening my heart to her dilemma, I ask gently, "Well, if you had to guess, what seems most likely to you?"

"I think," she responds, "that it has something to do with learning the real meaning of love." Part of me is excited that her intuition is working so well, but with restraint I remain quiet as she probes deeper within herself. "And truth . . . I deal with things so shallowly. I think part of my purpose is to see everything more clearly and learn to deal with things as they really are."

Getting Bigger

After a few more moments of silence, I quietly inquire, "Are you aware, Carol, of feeling any different now than when you came in here awhile ago?"

"Oh, yes—I feel as if a tremendous burden has been lifted off of my heart!" Great, I think: all this relaxation and we haven't even begun the bodywork. Sort of like an enzyme soak before doing the laundry.

"So what has happened?" I ask. Hopefully this will lead her to understand more distinctly the process that has resulted in this expanded state of awareness. Carol is sharp, and based on our past work together, it seems likely that she will be able to make the connections herself.

"Well, when I came in here I was obsessing about all of my problems, all of the conflicting things that I wanted. Then when you encouraged me to touch my deeper yearnings, my life's purpose, somehow I had to get bigger inside just to consider them. It's like I switched from pushing on the block of foam rubber to opening the walls of my mind. And now that I feel so much more spacious inside, I can see my problems from a different perspective." Carol pauses, grins, and says, "I'm not sure they're small enough to cover with a cloth and decorate with ornaments, though!"

Horizontal Desire Versus Vertical Aspiration

"Perhaps not yet," I reply to Carol, "but you're moving in the right direction. Sometimes it's helpful to have precise word tools to help us in this re-membering process. So how about if we agree that the word *desire* refers to the process of feeling some lack inside, imagining something that will satisfy that lack, and then trying to acquire it so you can feel satisfied. This is a horizontal process, and it can go on forever. If you look back on your own life, I think you'll see that getting what you wanted only brought satisfaction for a brief time and most always generated more desires in its wake. All desires keep you on the horizontal plane, in the world of duality, of lack and fulfillment. Of course it's important to become skillful operating on this level—that's called being 'grounded.' But in my experience, no amount of horizontal fulfillment *alone* brings long-term satisfaction. The horizontal plane is necessary for life, but it is hardly sufficient to fulfill our deepest longings.

"In contrast to this, let's use the words *yearning* or *aspiration* to refer to a vertical process. Yearning is aimed at some transcendent quality. It could be Spirit, God, the Source, your Buddha Nature, or one of the qualities associated with this transcendent state: Peace, Joy, Freedom, Love, and Truth are close English approximations.

"However you conceive of 'It,' though, the aim of true yearning lifts you out of the horizontal plane and gives you another dimension in your life, just as the lifting and spinning of a two-dimensional circle defines a three-dimensional space called a sphere. Spheres aren't just bigger circles; they are the opening of circleness into another dimension. Likewise, genuine aspiration for Love or Truth or God lifts you out of the bondage of desires and opens the yearning heart to the realm of its truest existence. This is the principle behind the old aphorism 'And the Truth shall set you free.'"

Longing for the Source

Carol has been soaking in these insights like a sponge, originally hard and dry, now soft and fairly saturated. Sensing that the dialogue is complete, we move on into the bodywork room and explore together the physical aspects of those rigidities that have tended to keep her consciousness horizontal. With her intensified yearning for the source of Love and Truth, though, the vertical lift is strong and old horizontal patterns of resistance and fear melt easily. The "enzyme presoak" has been wonderfully effective today, and I suspect that this "wash" is going to come out cleaner than Carol has experienced for many a year. . . .

When Carol and I meet a few weeks later, she describes how great she felt for a few days after leaving that session. Then, she says, the inevitable "down" arrived, but this time she felt more prepared and skillful as she used her new insights to keep coaxing back her heart's yearning for its true purpose and goal. Her problems still dogged her, occasionally even worse than before, but more and more she found herself prepared to handle them compassionately and wisely. She called upon her inner grandmother regularly and repeatedly reminded herself that it was this inner wisdom, this vertical lift out of the conflicts of the moment, that would help her. The unconscious repeating of old frustrating desire patterns was gradually losing its hold on her, and the radiant joy with which she shared all this was ample proof that our inner peace explorations were bearing sweet and nourishing fruit.

The Web of Life

Open your consciousness to the deep web of relationship that under-lies and interweaves all experienc-ing, all knowing. It is the web of life in which you have taken being and in which you are supported. Out of that vast web you cannot fall. No stupidity or failure, no personal inadequacy, can ever sever you from that living web, for that is what you are and what has brought you into being. Feel the assurance of that knowledge. Feel the great peace, rest in it. Out of that great peace, we can venture everything. We can trust. We can act.

—*Joanna Macy*

SEVEN

Piecing Together the Puzzle

Once upon a time (or was it only yesterday?) a harried mother was nearing the breaking point as Didi, her inquisitive young daughter, bombarded her with unending questions. Noticing a picture of the Earth on the cover of a magazine, she carefully tore it into dozens of jagged-edged pieces, mixed them up, and gave the improvised jigsaw puzzle to Didi to reassemble.

Thinking she had bought herself at least half an hour of quiet, the mother was startled when Didi returned a few minutes later with the picture intact.

"Look, Mommy, the world is back together," exclaimed Didi proudly.

Astounded, her mother couldn't help but ask, "How did you get it all back together so fast, Honey?"

"It was easy!" exclaimed Didi with a grin of delight. "At first I couldn't see how to make the pieces of the Earth fit together. Then I looked on the other side of the pieces, and there I saw parts of a person. It was much easier to put the person together, so that's what I did. And when the person came together, so did the Earth."

—Retold from a story in The Dragon
Doesn't Live Here Anymore *by Alan Cohen*

Outer Mirrors Inner

So often we are confronted with the seeming impossibility of making the world around us a decent place to live. Suffering of all kinds presents itself with increasing forcefulness, and a compassionate heart may at times feel overwhelmed. Some of us find ourselves working so hard trying to make things right "in the world" that we may miss the fundamental truth of this lovely parable.

One of the basic principles we have been exploring in this book is the way different parts of a whole mirror each other. Part of the work of inner peace facilitators is to help recipients experience the contractions of physical tissue that they perceive as tightness, soreness, or pain, and help them link these conditions with their corresponding mental and emotional contractions. Hopefully, this will deepen their awareness of how when one part of them changes (softens), the other parts do also.

Likewise, as facilitators of inner peace, part of our growth is discovering how changes within are eventually mirrored in changes outside of ourselves. Wisdom teachings from around the world capture this truth: "As you sow, so shall you reap," "The macrocosm mirrors the microcosm," "As within, so without," and "You perceive only what you are."

To the degree that this principle is true and we have verified for ourselves that outer "reality" actually is influenced by our inner reality, we can confidently "turn the pieces over" and complete the jigsaw puzzle of life in the world. We do this by learning to fit together the pieces of "the person" (oneself) on the other side.

Changing the World from Within

Regardless of whether we have proven the above principle true yet in our own lives, one fact is undeniably clear: our capacity to create meaningful and enduring change in anything or anyone outside of ourselves is dwarfed by our much greater ability to change ourselves. So why not "work with the puzzle" where our inherent abilities are the greatest? This means focusing our transformative energy first on the inner obstacles that separate us from our longed-for clarity, balance, and peace. It means *bringing the war back home.*

As we observe life outside of us, it is easy to see how ongoing battles between people, institutions, and traditions create tremendous suffering. Likewise, if we carefully observe our *intra*personal world, we will see the same kinds of struggles between parts of ourselves. I may identify with my mind and attempt to control or dominate my body and emotions, but whatever displeasure they feel in being treated this way is powerfully, intimately, neurologically fed back to the other parts of "me." Mind, *pretending* it is "me," can ignore this feedback, but only at the cost of later suffering, disease, and degeneration of the entire person. *Intra*personally, the message is clear: we are all in this together. Genuine peace and fulfillment are nurtured by acceptance of this reality and frustrated by its denial.

The same idea is found in most spiritual teachings, and in recent decades it is also earning respect within the world of secular thinking through the science of ecology. From physics, the hologram is often used as an appropriate model for this inherent interconnection of all existence. (In a hologram, any piece, no matter how small, contains the complete picture.) So intellectually, it is becoming easier to accept that everything is connected and that the actions of *any* part ultimately affect *every* part of creation. But for most of us, this is still just a theory and has not yet become a living foundation of our lives and decisions.

The mind boggles with the immensity of the world "out there." Limits of time, money, and energy ultimately frustrate even the greatest of worldly explorers, confining their lives to but a minuscule fraction of what this planet offers. No such limits exist for the inner explorer, though. And if the principle that the macrocosm mirrors the microcosm is true, then *everything* that exists can be accessed by doing one's inner work.

Our Inner Work

Inner work has many definitions, but perhaps the most universal might be expressed as "seeking, accepting, and integrating truth (or reality) as deeply as possible." While we may start our quest investigating our individual truths, eventually the boundaries of "me" become fuzzy and permeable. At times "me" may become so expansive that it includes "you," "her," "him," and "it" in an ecstatic awareness of "my" life as an inseparable part of an ecologically choreographed dance, the totality of which might be called Truth, Reality, or Creation.

(If you are wondering at this point whether you have somehow stumbled into a discourse on esoteric spirituality by mistake, hold on.

This "line of thinking" circles back and meets itself as a practitioner's hands address chronic constrictions on a client's body. But first, just a few more steps along the perimeter . . .)

The Five-Faceted Diamond

Truth, while always an elusive term to define, can be subjectively experienced as the other side of the coin of Peace. A better metaphor, though, might be a diamond with five shining facets. In addition to Truth and Peace, there are Love, Joy, and Freedom. To the degree that you have one facet of this diamond, you have them all. To the degree that you are resisting any facet, all the others maintain their distance.

Therefore, it really doesn't matter *which* facet you seek; the crucial factor is the sincerity and commitment *with which* you seek. Find one, and you'll have them all. In this context, old dictums such as "Be still and know" and "Seek the Truth, and the Truth shall set you free" have a direct bearing on inner peace. Knowing (Truth), Freedom, and Peace are facets of the same diamond; open your heart and receive any one of them, and you will find yourself overflowing with them all. This "overflow" is the most precious gift healing arts practitioners have to offer their clients.

The Healing Process

One of the core principles that has surfaced several times in this book is that the most fundamental "training" for inner peace facilitators is the work we have done inside ourselves discovering, accepting, and integrating (or reframing) *our own* obstacles to inner peace. This also means that our usefulness to others seeking *their* inner truth arises in proportion to the work we have done learning to "dance" gracefully with *our* inner truth. As discussed throughout this book, this dance is greatly facilitated by ongoing professional supervision (for practitioners) and personal therapy with a "senior" healing arts professional appropriate for our particular situation.

There are three aspects that require our attention in the truth-seeking or inner peace-finding process. We may experience each to some degree as we deepen our own inner awareness. One of the gifts we can offer ourselves and others is clear descriptions to assist in the skillful navigation through these processes. While there is nothing sacred about the particular words used, it *is* crucial to understand that all three parts of the process are necessary for the long-awaited Truth-Peace-Love-Joy-Freedom diamond to reveal itself fully within the heart.

"Seeing" and Safety

The first step in this process is characterized by words such as *seeking, discovery, seeing, uncovering,* and *perceiving.* This phase brings a fragment of truth out of hiding and into awareness, at least temporarily. It thins the wall of denial sufficiently so that what is really inside can be sensed and more consciously felt and experienced. For long-repressed trauma, this can be incredibly painful and usually needs to happen a little bit at a time.

Through the process of my own ongoing professional supervision, I have learned that a mistake I frequently make as a practitioner is encouraging clients to "see" what's obvious to *me* faster than what is right for *them.* This has the effect of "stopping the process," of shifting the focus away from the clients' inner struggles to discover their own truths and onto *my* already distilled wisdom. (And this is only one of many ways practitioners may inadvertently obstruct the healing process.) Because of this tendency, part of my ongoing inner work is to catch myself doing this and as quickly as possible regain my balance and intuitive centeredness. I can then refocus on holding open a shared space of safety and love that offers struggling clients tremendous support regardless of what comes into their consciousness in a particular session.

A crucial aspect of this first part of the process is to set the stage for acceptance by creating relationships that are as free as possible from judgment. Each one of us carries inside old (and usually unconscious) programming telling us what is and is not OK to feel, think, and be. Any inner truth not meeting this criteria is routinely screened out, denied, or perverted to somehow make it seem acceptable to this inner judge. So powerful is this pattern that if you are alert, you can often catch people unconsciously setting you up to reinforce their preconceived judgments about themselves. Such collusion, needless to say, does *not* support an open inquiry as to what's *really* going on inside.

A major gift we offer as inner peace facilitators is to model an attitude of receptivity to *whatever* is real inside. Even though we may have to set and maintain appropriate boundaries for its expression, it is crucial that we genuinely accept the right of each aspect of self to exist, be heard, and be respected, no matter how much it may deviate from one's higher values or cherished self-image.

Such unconditional acceptance by a facilitator is especially important in situations where painful memories of past trauma may be almost ready to come into consciousness, but have been habitually repressed with mental judgments about their utter unacceptability. If those of us who are practitioners can remember that these habits of prejudice (judging before the reality emerges) have protected our clients from overwhelming fear and shame for most of their lives, we are more likely to stay balanced and transmit a powerful respect for these blocks, even as our tender words and skilled hands seek to soften their grip and coax them into a relaxed trust that allows inner truth to emerge more easily.

Coaxing what's been hidden into awareness, though, is only part of the work. Even more important is preparing a receptive emotional environment so that what is revealed feels safe, cherished, and able to, in some sense, *breathe.* The situation is analogous to bringing a new life into the world. Simply getting the infant out of the mother is only part of the work; helping the child feel that she or he belongs here and is loved is vitally necessary if the child is to survive and thrive.

Unconditional Acceptance

Once the recipient's hidden awareness has been exposed to the outside, the work moves to the second phase: bathing it in unconditional love, acceptance, and appreciation of the trauma it went through to emerge. Success in creating and maintaining this climate of acceptance helps the newborn awareness stay "alive." Without ongoing acceptance, this awareness can easily drift back behind its old walls of denial.

In this part of the work, we might suggest that the person we are serving personify the newly emerged aspect of her or himself—maybe even give it a name like "Little Susi," "Little Billy," or "Frightened Child." Before the session ends, we might discuss ways to strengthen the link between day-to-day consciousness and this newly revealed, and often somewhat tentative, part of the inner self. One person may decide to take his "little boy" for ice cream; another might give her "little girl" a bubble bath; others may choose to experiment with inner child dialogues in a diary or journal. Regardless of how it is done, though, expanded consciousness needs to be grounded in *behavior* to insure its survival.

Integration: The Puzzle Becomes Clearer

Deepening the genuine acceptance of whatever has been "seen" prepares the way for the final phase: integration of the new information into the inner "family" of selves (inclusion of the new "part" into the whole). Like any new relationship, the "getting to know each other" process evolves in its own way and time. As this unique dance unfolds from the depths of our being, our grace in surrendering to its rhythm is profoundly affected by how "limber" we are spiritually, mentally, emotionally, and physically. And this is where multidimensional transformation-oriented bodywork is so valuable.

Oh, yes, there's another benefit also. Each time this process of seeing, accepting, and integrating occurs, another piece of the puzzle falls into place. Slowly, imperceptibly, the picture of the true person comes together. Even though it may take a long time to become clear, as the person comes together, the world comes together. And as each approaches wholeness, the natural Truth-Peace-Joy-Love-Freedom facets of the diamond of life shine more and more brilliantly. As we do this, we grow closer to fulfilling the ancient longing of the human heart and at last solving the puzzle of life.

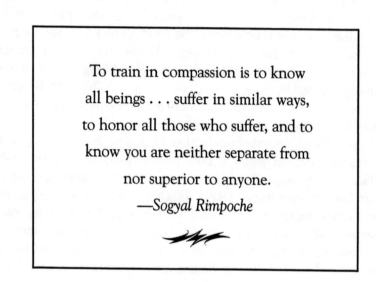

To train in compassion is to know
all beings . . . suffer in similar ways,
to honor all those who suffer, and to
know you are neither separate from
nor superior to anyone.

—*Sogyal Rimpoche*

Suffering and Joy

The Sufis have a saying that I keep in my interview room and share with clients when appropriate:

> Overcome any bitterness that may have come because you were not up to the magnitude of the pain that was entrusted to you. Like the Mother of the World who carries the pain of the world in her heart, each one of us is part of her heart and therefore endowed with a certain measure of cosmic pain. You are sharing in the totality of that pain. You are called upon to meet it in Joy instead of self pity. The secret is to offer your heart as a vehicle to transform cosmic suffering into Joy.

Three Orientations to Bodywork

There's that word again: *transform.* Why does it crop up so often in this book? And why would anyone in their right mind accept a calling to meet suffering with "Joy?" Is such a thing really possible for those of us not destined for sainthood?

Before tackling these megaquestions, let us backtrack a bit and start with an overview of the entire massage/bodywork field. As I understand it, there are actually three different orientations possible within this profession, each with its own model of reality, focus, goal, and purpose. Various techniques and modalities might be used within any of these categories. This way of looking at bodywork does not address what a practitioner *does* so much as the *attitude* or *approach* with which it is offered. As this field matures, healing arts professionals and touch therapists will hopefully develop greater clarity as to the uses, training, expectations, and limits appropriate for each.

- ❖ **The medical/remedial orientation** sees massage as an adjunct of medicine as generally practiced in the West. It shares the medical model of illness and is generally focused on "curing" bothersome symptoms. When the pain or dysfunctionality that brings the client has been eliminated or reduced as much as is thought possible, treatment is ended or moves into "maintenance." Many of these practitioners work with or take referrals from medical doctors and chiropractors, think in terms of "medical conditions," and speak medical language as transmitted in the curriculum of "approved" massage schools. Typical reasons for going to such a practitioner revolve around the idea "This will be helpful for my problem."
- ❖ **The relaxation/recreation orientation** focuses on enjoyment, sensual pleasure, and the temporary relief of muscular tension. It very much deals with the client feeling good *during* the session, as opposed to addressing factors that influence how they feel days *after* the session. This is the type of massage people might anticipate receiving at a spa or on a cruise ship. Typical reasons for having this kind of work center around the idea "I want to feel good."
- ❖ **The transformation orientation** may include aspects of either of the above, but it primarily seeks to influence and support long-term change in consciousness, physical structure, energy use, and/or other habit patterns. It is involved less with temporary "cures" (though clients generally feel better afterward) and more with revealing and releasing the *cause* of dis-ease, opening the door to true healing. (For additional discussion of *curing* versus *healing,* see chapter 4.)

Practitioners offering transformation-oriented bodywork might subscribe to any of several different models for understanding the nature of a client's physical, emotional, mental, and spiritual realities. Some cling firmly to one model, others are more eclectic, exercising their freedom to "mix 'n' match" from a variety of approaches. Clients drawn to this orientation would probably describe their motives for coming with phrases such as "learning about their blocks," "personal growth," and "releasing old stuff." Such clients may be incorporating a little bodywork along with other healing modalities, or they may use it as their primary "work" on their own path toward wholeness and inner peace.

Using this model that focuses on motivation rather than technique, let us now go back and explore the question raised at the beginning: Why would anyone . . . accept a calling to meet suffering with Joy?

Motivation

In the standard medical/remedial model, disease or pain is seen as "the enemy": the practitioner's skills are usually focused on destroying or eliminating whatever is understood to be the immediate cause of the problem. Yet this objectification of suffering as the enemy leaves little room for genuine understanding of and interaction with its deeper origins; meeting it with a vulnerable joy would be almost inconceivable.

In the relaxation/recreational model, the goal usually is to override suffering with pleasure—to at least temporarily replace the not-nice with something that *is* nice. This orientation sees suffering not as an enemy, but as something unpleasant and hence more or less to be ignored or overridden in the pursuit of pleasure.

To a transformation-oriented practitioner, however, the *roots* of suffering are of primary interest and concern. Not only is suffering not an enemy, but in this approach its wisdom and cooperation are actively sought. Suffering is understood to contain information about imbalance, about dis-ease that is crying for attention. It screams at us that things cannot go on the way they are. In suffering we are often more receptive to change, and sometimes it "makes us an offer we can't refuse."

Seeking the Wisdom in Suffering

One of the most precious fruits of a practitioner's own inner journey and intimate explorations in suffering is an ability to discriminate between the suffering that means *stop* versus the suffering that is a necessary, natural part of the healing process, is rich with potential wisdom, and leads eventually to greater freedom. For a transformation-oriented bodyworker, this hard-won ability is a trusted guide through the fogs of confusion into the clear light of Peace and—oh, there's that word again—Joy.

So you see how it comes together? First we must have done our own inner work sufficiently well to subjectively *know* the relationship between pain, acceptance, transformation, and Joy. Then it is not such a big leap to enter into the pain of another and, maintaining a vision of the Joy to come, court the wisdom buried deep behind decades-old walls of denial and terror.

Vulnerability

To be fully effective, this inner voyaging with another requires that we also be vulnerable—be open to experiencing the unknown and, at any moment, risk being confronted with our own undigested psychic material. The medical and the relaxation orientations to bodywork do not require this; their models allow clients to be dealt with as "other," allowing the practitioner to maintain a safe distance (usually) from the client's pain.

In transformation-oriented bodywork, though, such "safety" is seen as illusory. At any turn in the shared journey, either party is at risk for losing her or his balance, for being confronted with unwanted reflections of the inner self that must be handled with great skill and compassion. This is one reason why the discussion in this book comes back again and again to the importance of practitioners doing their own inner healing work as primary training for helping others to do theirs. Out of such work evolve tested and trustworthy habits for dealing with the unknown, which might include grounding through breath, regaining centeredness, witnessing energy inside and out, noticing—but not being dominated by—fear, being aware of our ignorance without intuition-blocking shame, reestablishing our connectedness with the planet, and prayer.

Those of us who are transformation-oriented bodyworkers and are operating as inner peace facilitators offer ourselves as guides, knowing that at any moment we risk stumbling into territory in which we ourselves are still strangers. Ironically, it is often at times such as these—when we are confronted before our clients by our apparent incompetence—that a new realm of trust and creativity can open between us, and the grace of healing flows abundantly for both.

Melting Inner Obstacles into Joy

So we come back to the question of motive and of whether we are truly willing to pay the price required to meet suffering with Joy. Or put differently, is our commitment to alleviate suffering, including our own, great enough to do *whatever it takes* to melt our own inner obstacles into Joy and repeatedly test this openness by exposing our vulnerability and Joy in the same crucible with our client's suffering?

Even if the answer to these questions is an enthusiastic "Yes!" we still must remember and honor our scope of practice. It is such a delicate dance: on the one hand we "dive in," trusting that good intentions, intuition, God's grace, or perhaps some luck will guide us through whatever arises. On the other we proceed cautiously, taking a seemingly endless number of tiny steps with our client, ever so slowly building up that fragile sense of trust and connection that is so crucial for this work.

At one moment we may feel expansive and confident, almost drunk from the distilled fruits of our own inner work. Yet in the blink of an eye we may find ourselves in unknown territory, feeling that our own insecurity and fear are a totally inadequate offering for this client clinging to us for guidance.

Then—and maybe only then—do we get to find out whether we contract, as we have from childhood, in reaction to what we desperately want to avoid. If so, we lose our access to Joy. For it is out of spaciousness—our fundamental balance—that healing compassion, patience, and Joy arise. When we become aware that we are contracting, we can accept this as a challenge to call upon our resources, recenter, and reconnect with our inner wisdom.

This process is certainly not always joyful, but our evolving skill and commitment will increasingly carry us through. We discover that as we regain our balance, Joy returns, though perhaps requiring of us an extensive exercise of patience first! We also learn that there are situations in which Joy can best express itself through gentle concern, patience, and compassion (which literally means "suffering together").

The Exquisite Dance

What an exquisite dance it is! Partly we come to meet our client's suffering in Joy, as a celebration of the gift—as the opening quote suggests—that has been entrusted to us by the "Mother of the World." Yet at the same time we expose our incompetence, our incompleteness, our vulnerability to losing our hard-earned balance and Joy. If we become too obsessed with trying to remember all the steps, we stumble over our own feet. If we get too unconscious merging with the music, we may well trample on our partner's feet.

With humble practice, balance *is* possible. And for those who truly are willing to become skilled partners in the dance of transforming suffering into Joy, Mother herself is the instructor. She presents herself in many ways: the still, small voice within, a flash of intuition, an experience of grace. As discussed previously, our task is to be willing and receptive students and to increase our skill in discriminating her guidance from the projections of ego.

The Example of Peace Pilgrim

For those of you who have not yet encountered her, I would like to introduce you to one of the clearest embodiments of Peace that has walked this planet in recent decades. Following an inner call at age forty, for the next twenty-eight years this formerly middle-class housewife traveled the highways of America until her death in 1981, walking until given shelter and fasting until given food. Abandoning her given name, she was known only as "Peace Pilgrim."

Peace (as her friends called her) is an inspiring fulfillment of the statement that began this chapter. Completely open to suffering, she regularly met it unflinchingly with Joy. Representing no religion, she transformed lives by sharing her transparent, living relationship with God and Love. Her message was simplicity itself:

> **This is the way of peace: overcome evil with good, falsehood with truth, and hatred with love.**

This can be the way of our work also. First in ourselves and then with our clients, the transformation goes on. The words may change to fit the situation, but the principles are the same: melt, dissolve, and transform (overcome) contracted consciousness and chronic tension (evil) with awareness, renewed flow of energy, and inner light (good); adaptive habits that protect us from pain (falsehood) with what is real inside (truth); and shame, unhealed wounds, and terror (hatred) with acceptance, balance, and peace (love).

For a copy of the booklet *Steps Toward Inner Peace*, which offers a brief introduction to Peace Pilgrim's life and teaching, you may write to Friends of Peace Pilgrim (see resources in chapter 21). I always keep a quantity of these booklets on hand to share with interested clients. Friends of Peace Pilgrim also offers a wonderful full-length book of her teachings, plus audio and videotapes and a wonderfully inspiring newsletter. There is no charge for anything they offer, though donations are welcome to pay production costs.

A Touch

A touch

may not mean much

in these days of tension . . .

and chronic fear . . .

and rush . . . rush . . . rush . . . !

Yet this I know :

    each time an inner child appears

    and asks for you with love;

    and gets instead a toy

    that has no warmth, that has no joy,

    something dies and rots.

    And once-cute little tots

    change into fearful, mean adults

    who worship naught in empty cults.

    And cry softly in their sleep,

    because their lovely child

    they could not keep.

A touch

may not mean much.

But it can say to your skin, "I'm here!

I have not left, I am quite near."

And if the touch could deeper go

down to the roots where tensions grow;
a passageway it would create
and weary darkness liberate.

Illustration by José Micaller

We are not gods, not yet at least.
But while we learn, let's soothe the beast.
If we can calm its running wild,
we just might find our inner child.

"Oh look!"
say hands with gentle touch,
"she smiled."

By facing fear are spirit warriors made;
Thus fear is naught of which to be afraid.
—E.J. Michael

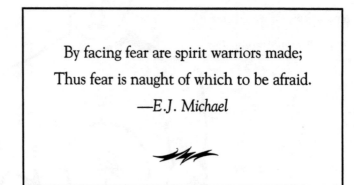

Working with the Inner Child

Each time an inner child appears
And asks for you with love;
And gets instead a toy
That has no warmth, has no joy,
Something dies and rots.
And once-cute little tots
Change into fearful, mean adults
Who worship naught in empty cults.
And cry softly in their sleep,
Because their lovely child
They could not keep.

Healing Old Wounds

One of the ways of understanding inner peace facilitation is as a form of alchemy. As practitioners begin working with clients, we are often faced with the reality of the poem above: with fearful, perhaps "mean" adults who have evolved habits over a lifetime to hide their awareness of pain once too terrible to accept. They assume they have lost their lovely child, and they may come to us with expectations no greater than temporary respite from their ongoing struggle in an inner world that "has no warmth, has no joy."

As our compassion offers softening and nurturing to that part of our client's inner landscape that is cold and joyless, we usually find that it is cluttered with the "toys" of the mind. These deep-rooted mental patterns deflect awareness away from feelings that the mind fears would

71

reveal too much and is terrified it would not know how to handle.

So gently we work with the wisdom that the words of author and teacher Stephen Levine express so well:

> Healing is an open book whose secret is that there is no secret at all. Healing uncovers the heart. . . . Investigation heals, because wherever awareness is focused, a natural balance eventually resumes. Healing follows awareness. Healing in the mind or the body follows the same path. First we acknowledge the pain. And soften to the hard places. . . . We change the direction from withdrawal to approach. It is a "reversal of fortune." Resistance dissolves into a willingness to heal . . . a direct entrance of awareness into the sensations in the area calling for healing. A brailling from moment to moment of the textures and changing forms we call sensations or pain. Exploring microscopically the moment-to-moment flow of consciousness in the body. Knowing the area "by heart.". . . Hard sensations softening at the edge. Dissolving in something even greater than our fear. Dissolving in the heart of the matter. Each sensation received as if it were an only child. Embraced tenderly by merciful awareness that seeks only its liberation.

Working at the Edge

As you read this quote, can you feel the ungraspable—yet very rich and real—edge between thinking and feeling, doing and being, healer and healing? Our adult minds so often crave understanding, demand to know *just what's going on here?* Yet when our clarity and compassion become an invitation to the terrified inner child to emerge into consciousness, we enter into a premental world, a reality more sensed than known.

Our role as inner peace facilitators requires us to maintain consciousness in two worlds simultaneously. We must "float" enough to enter into the confusing and, for the person we're helping, often unthinkable realm that traps the inner child in a distant *then*. Yet we also must remain solidly grounded in *this* moment, offering access to all the skills and wisdom we have acquired on our own journey toward freedom.

Then we are able to be a bridge between these two realms, demonstrating the possibility of being in two places at once; then what we *are* offers invitation and assistance according to the recipient's readiness.

Another function we provide as inner peace facilitators is defining and maintaining appropriate boundaries, both in our own inner process and in relationships with those we are serving. Boundary work is intimately related with feelings of safety, and this is vitally important for anyone opening a relationship with their inner child. Since much of the unhealed hurt from childhood arose from inappropriate (or nonexistent) boundaries, it is crucial that the process of reopening these old wounds be done in an environment of clear, respectful boundaries. This issue (which is discussed throughout this book, especially in appendix A) reveals its true importance only as we *personally experience* the safety of appropriate boundaries (or lack thereof) in our own healing work.

Looking Deeper Than Symptoms

Most bodywork practitioners have been taught to deal with the *symptoms* of wounds, not the wounds themselves. For example, when people come in after an accident, they receive massage work that softens the scar tissue forming around the injury. But how often do they also receive an appropriate environment for dealing with the more subtle, deeply held *feelings* that need a safe place to be processed in order to complete the healing process? The answer to this question is intimately connected to another one: How far have we, as inner peace facilitators, progressed in our own personal healing process?

When we notice symptoms in ourselves such as chronic muscle armoring, clinging to habitual defensive patterns, or an inability to feel safe for long in deep relaxation, these indicate that there are still inner wounds needing our compassionate attention. As we pursue healing—in ourselves or with a client—we discover that the process moves through three levels of gradually increasing freedom and awareness (as discussed in chapter 7).

Re-Membering

In the earlier stages of healing, we seek some kind of "re-membering," of reconnecting with a lost part (member) of ourselves that contains the information needed for full healing. What we can access at first may well be preverbal, so we open ourselves to heightened *feeling*. Undigested sensory memory may drift in and out of consciousness for a while, unsure if it is now safe to emerge.

One way to work with this tentative emergence of memory is to pretend that we (as the adults we are now) can somehow go back in time and physically hold and comfort the terrified little child we were at the time of the events that originally caused the wound. After all, who knows the needs of that little child better than we do? Opening our adult heart (as if we were this child's parent, friend, wise-person, aunt, uncle, or grandparent at that time), we may be able to directly experience how the pain associated with the wound was so overwhelming that the only way the child was able to cope at the time was to "shut down," to disassociate from the memory and deny that anything had happened. As a loving "big person," we bathe this child in unconditional acceptance and love, repeating over and over that whatever happened, our love still continues.

To the degree that we have done this work ourselves, we can coach others through the process, sometimes to the accompaniment of tears, irrational fear, or intense anger. And because those we're helping probably won't be able to proceed through this unknown and fearful inner space without confidence in our skillful assistance, we must develop and maintain strong links to an inner guidance or wisdom that does not fail us when the going gets tough.

As an inner peace facilitator, I *often* feel that I'm only one step ahead of the person I'm helping. Occasionally I have to limit our work in a session until I have had an opportunity to deepen *my* explorations through additional healing work of my own. This might include professional supervision, meditation, counseling, journal writing, yoga, or any of the other processes that support my personal growth.

So the first part of this healing cycle involves moving through habitual denial and lovingly, nonjudgmentally being with the inner pain. As this "being-with" process reveals more and more of the repressed truth within, acceptance can gradually evolve: *Yes, this really did happen. Yes, who I am really does include this pain.* Finally, re-membering—and loving acceptance of this previously exiled "member"—makes possible a genuine release, a letting go that had been impossible until the inner hurt was experienced and accepted. This "letting go" might mean the disappearance of bothersome symptoms, or it might simply offer enough spaciousness inside so that the trauma—and its residual symptoms—can be more deeply accepted and integrated. This may or may not bring *curing* of the symptoms, but it will always bring *healing* and the peace that comes with it. And in peace, there arises a mighty power for both acceptance and change.

A Zen Story

There is a lovely story from the Zen tradition that illustrates the above point beautifully. A distraught mother visits the town monastery and asks the abbot to talk to her son about his smoking habit. The abbot considers her request, and finally he tells her to bring the boy to him in two weeks' time. The mother thanks him and returns two weeks later with her son in tow. The abbot and the boy go for a walk together, and upon returning the boy announces that he is giving up smoking. The mother is delighted, but she can't resist drawing the abbot aside and asking, "Why did you ask me to wait two weeks before you would speak with my son?" The abbot looks to the ground and humbly replies, "When you came to me the first time, I, too, was a smoker. In order to speak to your son with integrity, I first had to become free of the habit myself."

Freeing Ourselves

Thus we see in so many ways that the crucial factor for competence as inner peace facilitators is how deeply we have worked with our own habits of fear and the constrictions of consciousness, heart, and tissue that this addiction inevitably brings. To the degree that we as healing humans "do our work" and expand the space inside that is no longer resisting chronic hurt through denial, judgment, and clinging, we as increasingly skillful inner peace facilitators will see this freedom reflected in the level of acceptance and safety that we are able to offer others. The old adage applies: "It takes one to know one." Having developed familiarity with the confusion and drama of the inner child's realm through our own personal work, we are then more able to skillfully guide others through their similar as yet undiscovered territory.

As we continue our quest for inner truth and freedom, our tree of experience will bear refreshing fruits for both ourselves and those around us. The more sincere we are, the greater the likelihood we will become more humble, both personally and as inner peace facilitators. We humans are so tempted to present ourselves as more "whole" than we actually are! Ongoing self-confrontation work undercuts this shiny facade and leaves us interacting as one wounded—and healing— human being with another.

Also, from "doing the work" ourselves, we are able to explore with and explain to others from firsthand experience rather than just "book learning," which is so often less than satisfactory. And we may well find that our own inner work has opened channels of empathy and compassion for those we serve that were inaccessible until we learned how to give this same compassion to our own wounded inner child.

The problems that exist in the world
cannot be solved by the level of thinking
that created them.
—*Albert Einstein*

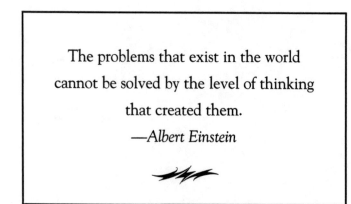

What Is Inner Peace?

If peace of mind is your goal,
    look for errors in your beliefs and expectations.
        Seek to change them, and not the world.
           And always be prepared to be wrong.
But if being right is your goal,
    you will find the error in the world,
        and seek to change it.
           But don't ever expect peace of mind.
              —Peter Russell, author of
              The Global Brain *and* A White Hole in Time

Peace and Healing

In our culture, health is usually understood to be the absence of dis-ease and peace the absence of conflict. However, many of us are awakening to the reality that true health and true peace are much more than the absence of their opposite. In chapter 4 we discussed healing as investigating and changing dis-ease at its source versus curing as merely the suppression of symptoms. The same idea applies to peace, which in its deeper meaning refers to the result of healing—of experiencing, accepting, and allowing change at the root source of dis-ease.

A person who is filled with vibrant, glowing health is fundamentally different from a person who is barely "not sick." Likewise, the person who is centered in a spacious peacefulness—hard won by dealing with "errors in [his or her] beliefs and expectations"—is fundamentally different from the person who is enjoying a pause (or suppression) of inner turmoil. Enduring peace involves an *increase of awareness*; this is the opposite of the relative peace that results from blocking awareness of painful truths.

We have discussed many "painful truths" that through our denial or inability to work with them are the cause of our reduced consciousness. Some of these include unresolved inner child trauma, personal-value conflicts, religious distortions of God, and a commercial culture that promotes superficiality and fear in order to feed its economic engines.

Buddha's Four Noble Truths

Are there any fundamental principles that underlie all of these sources of suffering? Twenty-five hundred years ago a simple spiritual seeker thought so. After much rigorous "research" in the laboratory of his heart, he—who had earned the name Buddha ("awakened one")— came to understand and share what are now called the "Four Noble Truths." These arise out of an awareness that there are two different *somethings* inside that both claim to be "me." While different traditions give them different names, for now let us call them Spirit—the eternal soul, spark of God, or truth that is the core of our existence—and ego or personality—who we usually think we are.

The First Noble Truth says that identifying with our personality is the root cause of all suffering. The personality is seen as a projection from and a limitation of our true self. A useful analogy derives from movie projection. The film in the projector represents the personality. Movie film filters the light behind it, creating an ever-changing pattern of drama on the screen. Likewise, the personality acts as a filter on the light of the spirit, projecting unending dramas onto the screen of the mind.

Movies from the Mind

Think about it: all the movies you have ever seen—comedies or tragedies, exciting or boring, inspiring or degrading—have one thing in common. If you trace the images on the screen back to their source, into the projection booth and behind the constantly moving frames of film, all movies originate from a point of pure white light. Generally we are not interested in pure light; we pay our money to see *drama,* to experience dancing *limitations* of light. And there is nothing wrong with this as long as we remember that it is only a movie—it is not real. But if someone becomes addicted to movies and refuses to ever leave the darkness that is required for such fantasies to be enjoyed, then we call them "mentally ill."

In a similar manner, the Buddha saw that becoming addicted to (and believing in the reality of) the movies in our mind—"me"—is the fundamental error out of which all suffering grows. From this follows the Second Noble Truth: Suffering is a self-created result of our desires. Again, consider the simple logic of this. If my true nature is completeness (analogous to white light, which contains all colors within it), then on this level there can be nothing that I lack. But when I shift my attention to the screen, when I identify with the movies of my personality rather than the spirit (completeness) that is their source, then I am no longer all colors; lack becomes real, and desire for what is perceived as lacking can arise.

Desire and Suffering

In a sense, when we desire anything, we are sensing a part of ourselves that through the process of mental movie making has been filtered out—has become a separate something "out there." So actually, all desire is an attempt to be whole, to re-member our white-light nature by grasping at flickering colors on the screen of life. But since the colors we really want were "lost" back in the projection booth, struggling to attain them on the screen is inherently an exercise in futility. Our efforts must always meet sooner or later with frustration and, hence, suffering.

The Third Noble Truth states what the analogy above implies: that desire and its inherent suffering are unnecessary. Then in the Fourth Noble Truth, the Buddha describes an eightfold path for awakening from our addiction to the dream (movies), thus ending our own suffering and making it possible for us to meaningfully help all other sentient beings awake also.

Desire Versus Aspiration

To more deeply understand the wisdom of these truths, it is important to differentiate between what is called *desire* here and what might be termed *aspiration* (see chapter 6). One way of looking at these is that desire is a horizontal energy, and aspiration is a vertical one. In desire, we seek something on the level of mind or matter. Desire is personality feeling a lack, finding something it imagines will fill that lack, and then seeking to possess or attain this object of desire. There is, of course, a period of happiness that occurs when the object is obtained, but the cycle always continues. Soon another desire will come up, and there will be tension as we strive to fulfill this desire and then temporary relaxation when the fulfillment occurs. Like a dog chasing its tail, we may travel a good many miles, but we never get anywhere.

Aspiration, on the other hand, is a vertical movement. In the sense that it is being used here, aspiration always seeks something transcendent, a principle or truth that is inherently more than our personality can imagine. Aspiration is for Light (in the analogy above), for the source of our existence. Since the Source, God, or Truth is beyond anything our mind can imagine, we often seek one or more of its attributes, which include Love, Truth, Joy, Freedom, and Peace.

Awakening Breath

The very process of aspiring lifts us out of the circular, horizontal realm of our inner movies. Just as opening the back door of a movie house on a sunny day floods the screen with sunlight and washes out the movie, making it no longer interesting, so does genuine aspiration reduce the addictive quality of our inner dramas as it heightens our longing to reconnect with Spirit, the Source, or God.

The word *aspire* is part of an important family of words growing out of the Latin *spirare*, meaning "to breathe." In Sanskrit, the word for breath (*prana*) also means "life force." *To aspire,* then, means to breathe upon, to focus one's life force upon the highest, upon the Source. Linguistically related to this are *inspiration* (to breathe in, to be nurtured by taking in a vision or aspect of the Source) and *conspiracy* (several people breathing together, pooling their life force in the service of some purpose greater than any one of them).

Changing Our Level of Thinking

Albert Einstein said, "The problems that exist in the world cannot be solved by the level of thinking that created them." Likewise, the problems created by the ego or personality cannot be truly solved by the limited consciousness of that personality. To *desire* a solution to suffering has no meaning; to *aspire* changes our level of thinking. Aspiration lifts consciousness above the level of thought and into the realm of direct perception. Here, we *know*. This is the realm from which intuition arises and "speaks to us" in our mental world. But the *knowing* of genuine intuition is who we truly are, not the confusing and suffering-producing patterns whirling on the screen of the mind. So, actually, when we aspire, we are yearning for our own true self, for the original light out of which comes all these dramas, pleasures, frustrations, and limitations.

The Still Mind

Another great thinker who wrote extensively about these matters, J. Krishnamurti, said, "When the mind is still, tranquil, not seeking any answer or solution even, neither resisting nor avoiding, it is only then that there can be regeneration, because then the mind is capable of perceiving what is true, and it is the truth that liberates, not our effort to be free." In other words, it really doesn't matter how much we *think about* suffering, the Noble Truths, peace, or expanded consciousness. What is needed is a *direct experience* of these realities, an experience that is by its very nature inaccessible to mind—and, alas, also inaccessible to anyone who has completely identified with her or his mind. This is why meditation (quieting-the-mind practice) is so important.

Navigating Our Way Toward Peace

Notice how compassionate the universe is. When such mental identification becomes chronic, when our identification with mind's limited consciousness cuts us off more and more from Joy, Love, Freedom, Truth, and Peace, which are our true nature, then suffering comes. If we are wise, we allow suffering to "shake up" our too-tight world. As the opening quote suggests, we "look for errors in [our] beliefs and expectations" and seek to change *them*—not the world. Yet our minds seem to constantly argue that the source of our suffering is "out there" in the world.

"And always be prepared to be wrong." This attitude is a prerequisite for the genuine aspiration that leads to lasting freedom. For what else is there to be free from but our own clinging to wrong ideas and behaviors? As it is used here, *wrong* is not a moral word—it does not refer to good or bad. Rather, it is a navigational tool. Just as a mariner seeking the shortest path across the ocean uses a compass and sextant, so do we who aspire to identify more fully with the realm of Love, Truth, Freedom, Joy, and Peace use this goal as our magnetic north or pole star. As a sailor from America to Europe seeks to maintain a course of due east and views all other settings as wrong *for that voyage,* so do we follow our conscience (inner compass) and intuition, gradually learning to interpret the force of desires as "wrong" insofar as it leads us in any direction other than that of our heart's deepest longing.

This skillful navigation is another way of talking about successful inner peace facilitation. Valuable tools to assist us are these previously mentioned principles: as within, so without; the macrocosm mirrors the microcosm; as we sow, so shall we reap. The more experienced and successful we become in perceiving and following our own inner guidance, the more we will have to offer others as their inevitable dramas, traumas, and forceful desires seem to blow them any which way but east. To the degree that our hard-earned skills as inner voyagers and our aspiration for Truth, Love, Freedom, Joy, and Peace keep our own course true, we can provide something of enduring value as we enter into an *aspirational conspiracy* with others who, having floundered long enough at sea, are ready to accept guidance and inspiration. Together we share the breath, the life force, and the vision that keep us on course. And, mysteriously, we often discover that such a conspiracy even invites the winds of fate to assist us on our journey Home.

I have three treasures:
Love, Frugality, and Humility.
Having Love, I can be courageous.
Being Frugal, I can afford to be generous.
Being Humble, I can learn
the wisdom of the world.
—*Tao Te Ching*

ELEVEN

Working with the Questions

Our Quest for Balance

A sojourner on a long journey found herself lost in an immense forest. After seemingly endless wandering, she came across the cottage of an old woman who was sitting on her front step knitting.

"Dear friend," said the traveler with relief, "I am so very lost. Won't you please show me the way?"

"Well, now, that all depends on where are you going," said the woman, smiling sweetly at the weary traveler and offering her some water.

"I . . . I . . . why, I can't seem to remember."

"Well, then," said the old woman with a twinkle in her eye, "if you don't know where you're going, it really doesn't matter how you get there."

Where Are You Going?

This story illustrates the predicament so many of us find ourselves in these days. All around us voices clamor, "More!" "Faster!" "Harder!" as if these somehow pointed the way out of the pervasive sense we find growing deep inside us that *something is not right.* There is an almost unquestioned assumption in our culture that whatever the ailment, consuming some product, service, or experience will make us feel better.

So most of the time we are leaning into the future, projecting our expectations of contentment into the next workshop, the new home, increased business, or perhaps a budding relationship. And, indeed, these *do* fulfill us for a time. But they extract a price: our balance. Always yearning for the future or grasping to hold on to the past, we gradually forget the experience of peace, of being content in the present.

Without inner peace, which is the foundation of any enduring happiness, sooner or later the hunger returns, another apparent "solution" presents itself, and we're off again, into another cycle of hunger, consumption, temporary satisfaction, and then, inevitably, more hunger. The moments of satisfaction, while often incredibly sweet, are always over much too soon. So we spend most of our energy trying to "get there again" or else reliving the happiness of times past. In other words, we are almost never balanced in the moment.

I personally find it almost impossible to deal skillfully with these forces unless I return to the core questions life presents to us: Who am I? Why am I here? What is the purpose of my life? Even if we are not sure of our answers, just sincerely grappling with the questions forces us to expand our consciousness in the present moment. In this spacious *now*, there's a chance that we can see the past and future, desire and fulfillment—*all* pairs of opposites—in a way that reveals their true nature and deprives them of their apparent power to pull us off center.

The Ego Equation

There's a lovely little equation that captures this idea beautifully:

$$\text{Consciousness} = \frac{1}{\text{Ego}}$$

In this equation, the term *ego* refers to *who we think we are;* it is what we mean when we say "I." Consciousness is the ability to perceive what really is. Even though these concepts are not quantifiable, this equation suggests the relationship between ego and consciousness.

So according to this equation, when we think, *I'm great,* consciousness becomes quite tiny. But as ego diminishes, consciousness grows. For instance, if ego were to shrink to a tenth of what it had been, consciousness would increase ten times; if ego diminished to a minuscule millionth of what it had been, consciousness would expand a millionfold. And in the moment of ultimate realization, when we directly and fully experience that the meaning of "me" is zero, we enter into a mathematical anomaly. Perhaps you remember learning in high school algebra that any number divided by zero is infinity. It is a phenomenon that lies outside of "normal" mathematics, yet this relationship of zero and infinity is inherent in its very foundation.

Likewise, unbound consciousness, while outside of the reality we consider "normal," is a *potential that is fundamental to our existence*. Of course, we can't prove this from direct experience until "me" diminishes to zero. The formula, though, doesn't demand ultimate surrender to give results. It predicts—and we can verify this in our own experience—that every time we become less absorbed in our own desires or fears, there will be a corresponding increase in our awareness of truth, of the way things really are. Likewise, the formula also predicts that whenever we become lost in our emotions, cravings, or personal concepts (increasing our absorption in "me"), our consciousness will shrink. This leaves us feeling less secure in life and more deprived, and it intensifies the clinging to ego's reality as "all I can be sure of," thereby shrinking consciousness even further. It is the ultimate vicious cycle.

This may sound terribly philosophical, but I encourage you to consider whether it offers an accurate explanation for what we are observing all over the world in recent years. As people place their focus more and more on themselves (or a collective "ego" such as a religion, nation, or ethnic group), consciousness everywhere has been contracting. This causes us to be collectively myopic, abusive to others, and disrespectful of our planet—perhaps even to the point of destroying her ability to sustain our lives. And as we perceive what we're doing, our fear and guilt inflame ego ever further, contracting consciousness to the point where we can barely find the will to change.

If we do choose to change, though, what can we do to lift ourselves and others out of this chronic and increasingly destructive cycle of inflamed ego and contracted consciousness? One way of working with this question is to remember how we first began losing our precious inner balance. This might arise from psychological investigations, spiritual practices, contemplation, experiences in nature, discussions with friends—the *how* isn't nearly so important as the sincerity and commitment of the inquiry.

The Pull of Opposites

Another approach to retrieving balance is to explore the dichotomies in our lives, the unresolved inner conflicts that seem to tug us in opposing directions. (Such investigations become especially important for healing arts practitioners attempting to clarify their feelings and policies concerning financial accessibility for their clients; see part 4.) Some of these conflict pairs include affluence versus austerity, needs versus desires, value versus worth, and human happiness versus divine joy.

Affluence Versus Austerity

In an article by architect Tom Bender (published in *In Context* magazine, issue 37, and adapted from his book *The Heart of the Place*), affluence and austerity are explored in an unusual light:

> The luxuries of simple living are closer to being soul-satisfying and life-enriching. We've invested in friends instead of stocks. We watch the sunset and moonrise instead of TV. We make music instead of consuming it.
>
> We still have had to take care of dirty baby bottoms and all the other maintenance work of living. But those chores of everyday living return to us a deepening, and give us unexpected nurture for new experiences. . . .
>
> What we were learning was the real meaning of *austerity*. Austerity does not exclude richness or enjoyment. What it does do is help us avoid things that keep us from our goals in life.
>
> Affluence has a real cost. Its possibilities demand impossible commitments of time and energy. It fails to discriminate between what is wise and useful and what is merely possible. We end up foregoing the things necessary for a truly satisfying life to make time and space for trivia. Like a garden, our lives need to be weeded if they are to produce a good crop.

Needs Versus Desires

Discriminating between needs and desires is a similar process to that of weeding a garden. As the "ego equation" above demonstrates, the more we focus on our desires—which intensifies ego—the more we eventually contract our consciousness. But being "selfless" to the point of not eating well or taking care of other inherent needs obviously does not work either. So we inquire, What—for me, at this time—is the boundary between *genuine* need and ego-gratifying desire?

I personally believe that the answer is unique for each of us and that it may change from situation to situation. We work with this question not to attain an "answer," but rather as a way of expanding our consciousness. This, according to the equation, must eventually reduce ego, which simultaneously reduces desire. And as desire diminishes, the question becomes less relevant. So in a strange way, we must work with the question in order to transcend the question.

Value Versus Worth

Considering worth versus value provides some fascinating insights as we become more conscious of how we use our limited financial resources. It's also crucial for healing arts practitioners as they formulate financial accessibility policies and decide with whom they will share their skills professionally.

According to the dictionary, *value* means fair or proper equivalent in money, while *worth* refers to the quality of a person, object, or experience and is measured by the esteem in which it is held. Webster says these terms may be used interchangeably when applied to the desirability of something material (an ounce of gold *valued* at three hundred dollars is *worth* three hundred dollars).

In dealing with less-tangible attributes, though, such as healing services, the two terms have different meanings. Worth refers to something *intrinsic* in what is being offered. Value, on the other hand, compares various offerings in a marketplace and assigns them a *relative* monetary significance. The example used in the dictionary is that the true *worth* of Shakespeare's plays cannot be measured by their *value* to the commercial theater. (This and other financial issues are explored more fully in appendix B.)

Happiness Versus Joy

The question of happiness versus Joy brings us full circle back to the original questions: Who am I? What is my purpose in life? If "I" is identified with ego—with the limited consciousness that is my personality—then trying to get as much happiness as possible makes a lot of sense. But if our reason for living has more to do with increasing consciousness and deepening our direct experience of Truth and Reality, then pursuing happiness or avoiding pain become secondary—even rather uninteresting—goals. Consciousness and Truth are their own rewards—and they are synonymous with Joy. Once a taste for Joy is developed, the hunger for mere happiness soon fades.

Balance and Enduring Peace

The process of grappling with these questions confronts us with our own unique ways of contracting our consciousness—with those personal mental habits that deprive us of the inner balance that is a prerequisite for enduring peace. As we work with these questions, it is important not to get lost in shame about the past or guilt because we fall so far short of our highest ideals. We may need to remind ourselves that their purpose is to bring us back to center, to reveal how off balance we have become in thinking about "me," and then to refocus on our greater, more inherently rewarding life goal, Consciousness, and its inherent Joy, Peace, Love, Freedom, and Truth.

As we work with life's core questions for our own inner reasons, it becomes increasingly easier to hear how we are called to behave in relation to others, especially those we serve. As this "dance" between my consciousness and another's grows more spacious and graceful, it naturally becomes much more fulfilling in and of itself. Practitioners, for instance, may well find that financial issues in their lives and with their clients diminish in importance. Those who dare to test this may joyfully discover most of their clients paying as much as they can *without* rigid financial policies, and both client and practitioner may both end up laughing as they realize how totally inadequate *any* payment is relative to the true *worth* of what they have shared together.

Oh, yes, in case you haven't already proven this for yourself, laughter is a magnificent way to regain your balance. And Peace. And Joy.

Until one is committed there is hesitancy, the chance to draw back, always in effectiveness. Concerning all acts of initiative (and creation), there is one elementary truth the ignorance of which kills countless ideas and splendid plans: that the moment one definitely commits oneself, then providence moves, too. All sorts of things occur to help one that would never otherwise have occurred. A whole stream of events issues from the decision, raising in one's favor all manner of unforeseen incidents and meetings and material assistance, which no man could have dreamt would have come his way. I have learned a deep respect for one of Goethe's couplets: "Whatever you can do, or dream you can, begin it. Boldness has genius, power, and magic in it."

—W.H. Murray

TWELVE

Tips and Techniques

In this chapter we will briefly explore several topics, any one of which could inspire a full book by itself. Also included are recommendations of several books that I have found useful in developing my own understanding.

Victim Thinking Versus Responsibility

In my discussions with clients, very often they will describe their experiences as *victims* of someone else. It is often helpful to open a dialogue concerning the nature of victim thinking and to explore together its advantages and disadvantages for the client.

For instance, when we believe we are victims, we are not responsible for our suffering; we see the source of our pain as "out there," and thus we are both innocent and helpless in relationship to it. This belief in innocence gets us off the hook, but it also denies that we have much power to meaningfully change the situation. Hence we live in continuing fear that we might be victimized again.

To the degree that we have successfully navigated the maze of victim thinking in ourselves, we can guide our clients through an exploration of their conflicting beliefs in this delicate yet powerful topic. Supporting ideas include the law of cause and effect (which almost no one will deny) and how this universal principle might be applied to help clients reframe and more broadly understand their roles as victims and any hidden factors behind their apparent innocence.

This is very tricky business. With one false move, a facilitator can easily fall into a judgmental stance that then intensifies the client's defenses. Through personal anecdote, though, we can often demonstrate how accepting and realistically working with a sense of personal responsibility ("I am the cause of my own experience of life") is hard work emotionally, but ultimately pays off handsomely in an increased sense of freedom, safety, and peace.

The Meaning of Forgiveness

Another powerful approach for this kind of dialogue is exploring the meaning of forgiveness. Crucial here is the idea that forgiveness does *not* mean that what someone did was OK. It does mean, though, that for our own inner peace we choose to let go of the hardness, judgment, and blame that we have been carrying. For an excellent book on this topic, see *Forgiveness: A Bold Choice for a Peaceful Heart* by Robin Casarjian.

Exploring Authority

A topic closely allied with victimhood and responsibility is that of authority. In childhood most of us learn that authority lies "out there." As we grow toward adulthood, we usually either internalize our outer authorities (parents, church, teachers) or else rebel against them. Yet this rebellion is actually a negative (or reverse) acceptance of an outer authority or source of guidance. Outer authority still determines our decision-making process, though we may feel as if we are rejecting it with an attitude that proclaims, "If *you* say 'do this,' I'll make sure I do the opposite!"

As inner peace facilitators, we may sometimes see these patterns acted out in relationships with us. Often we are seen as "the authority," and there is some attempt to mold behavior according to our guidance. Sometimes we are seen as an authority to rebel against, even when what we are attempting to teach is exactly what the other person most deeply wants.

Part of our work, then, is to help others claim authority in their own lives and become more skillful in accessing their own sources of wisdom within. Such techniques as exploring a situation to emphasize new self-empowering possibilities (reframing) support this goal, as does a sense of humility and coseeking on the part of the facilitator. Those of us who are bodyworkers can help clients move from an attitude of "I am *getting* a massage" to a more participative approach such as "I am learning about the emotions stored in my body and using this session to practice feeling and releasing the chronic tensions that limit my freedom."

Prayer and Healing

An excellent book for inner peace facilitators is Larry Dossey's *Healing Words: The Power of Prayer and the Practice of Medicine.* As a highly accomplished and respected mainstream physician, Dr. Dossey summarizes hundreds of research projects that scientifically demonstrate that focused intention (prayer) can affect medical outcomes in another person. Of special interest is his exploration of how the beliefs and attitudes of a healing professional affect the client's healing process.

"Cooking" Appropriately for Each Client

How we share our healing abilities and wisdom with others is often more important than what is actually given. A lovely story from India illustrates this point:

> A mother goes to the market and buys a fine fresh fish to feed her family. For her sickly father-in-law, she makes a thin soup from the head. For her laborer son, she fries a filet and serves it with a rich sauce. For the young children, cleverly designed fish sticks are baked and gently seasoned. And for her beloved mother, who loves spicy foods, a pungent curry is prepared. From one fish, four different meals are prepared, each given according to the digestive capacities of the recipient.

Sharing our gifts with others, then, involves accurately appraising their ability to absorb and integrate. Offer too much and it goes over their heads; assume too little capacity and we can easily end up sounding condescending. It's also important to remain vigilant in these appraisals, as another's capacity may vary from moment to moment and session to session.

Perception Versus Projection

We have often discussed the importance of intuition or inner guidance. Inherent in this approach to healing is our ongoing commitment to discriminating more and more deeply between actual *perception* (of inner wisdom, God's guidance, etc.) and often confusing *projections* (arising from ego, unconscious desires, hidden fears, etc.) This discernment is a central concern of any life devoted to serving or being a clear channel for a higher power. Regular personal-growth and spiritual-unfolding practices are crucial until the fog of our personality has been completely dispelled by the light of truth.

Such practices include meditation; professional supervision and/or ongoing personal counseling; physical-consciousness development such as hatha yoga, t'ai chi ch'uan, or martial arts; dream work; journal writing; and personal-growth workshops. Also important is ample time to contemplate, digest, and integrate all you are discovering in these practices.

Inner Child Family Therapy

The fields of family therapy, gestalt therapy, and psychosynthesis offer wonderful suggestions for how we can help others reorganize their constricted emotions and the resulting mental and physical tension patterns. One approach I love to explore with those who are receptive is a concept from the family therapy orientation: When one member of a family "has a problem," it can be fully dealt with only by treating the entire family unit.

Combining this principle along with the idea that each of us is made up of many subpersonalities (inner children, internalized mother, etc.), we can invite those we are assisting to recognize and name each member in their own inner family. We can even support them in having dialogues between inner members, bringing to light their fears, grievances, and yearnings.

A simple technique for this kind of investigation is to imagine, for instance, an inner child sitting on an empty chair nearby. The "adult" could then be invited to speak to that child, venting frustrations, blames, and fears about how this child hurts or limits the adult's life. When this monologue is complete, the speaker physically moves over into the child chair and is invited to *become* the child for a while and talk back to the adult self. As facilitators, we help create a safe environment for this dialogue, offer suggestions to each as to what the other might need to hear, and suggest appropriate times for switching positions.

In many situations, I have seen tremendous softening on all levels occur this way before a single physical touch has been given. After such an inner dialogue, massage can be a soothing, integrating, and life-affirming part of a deeply healing experience. A reminder, though: such dialogues can easily release strong, previously repressed feelings. It is crucial that if you are inviting such a release, you are able to lovingly and skillfully stay with, accept, and guide whatever arises. Needless to say, the degree to which you've integrated such inner explorations in your own life will determine your competence in facilitating such work in another.

Welcoming Chaos

Another book that can profoundly expand and enhance our under-standing of what we might offer as inner peace facilitators is *Leadership and the New Science* by Margaret J. Wheatley. While designed for man-agement consultants and organizational leaders, this wonderfully writ-ten and well-researched book explains clearly how our limited (and sometimes erroneous) understanding of scientific principles has led to psychological and organizational theories that are of limited usefulness for today's challenges. Since part of what we can offer as inner peace facilitators is support for understanding and working with inner con-flicts, tensions, and constrictions in new and more freeing ways, the material in this book is easily applicable in our work as well.

One of the core principles Wheatley explores is chaos and how it has been understood both by academic physics and by organizations and individuals in the process of transformation. The very word implies *out of control*, yet this is not its meaning in contemporary physics. Chaotic phenomena are lawful, though not precisely predictable in the way the motion of gears in a clock is predictable. Chaos increases when the energy flowing through a system (or person) is greater than the struc-ture of that system is used to. Because chaos forces us into unknown ter-ritory, we usually fear it. What this book demonstrates, though, is that chaos is much more understandable than we might have believed. It also contains within its unpredictability the seeds of new, unimagined ways of being that can successfully integrate our currently unmanageable problems into a higher level of consciousness.

Sound familiar? Whether one is providing transformative assistance to General Motors or Jane Doe, the principles are remarkably similar. Move past denial (see what's actually there), accept this new, more comprehensive information (even though it is frightening and feels chaotic), and then be open to discovering new ways of integrating (organizing) this expanded reality for the greater good of all concerned. (This principle, as applied to inner peace facilitation, was discussed in detail in chapter 7.)

Chaos theory is a vast and often challenging area of study, and these few paragraphs cannot begin to give even the briefest sketch of its importance and power. Wheatley, however, provides an introduction to this concept with warmth, delight, and numerous examples of its applicability to the challenges we face daily.

If you wish to live in the light,
you must step out of the shadows.
—E.J. Michael

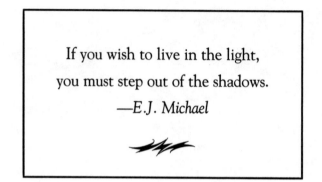

THIRTEEN

The Challenge of Year-End Holidays

Client Notes
December 16, 4:30 p.m.

Cindy B. has just left after her fourth session here. I thought we were making such wonderful progress in helping her learn to relax more deeply and handle her chronic tension in more creative ways. But today she was almost unreach-able. Talking endlessly about how she was never going to be able to finish everything she had to do before Christmas, Cindy seemed sealed away in a world of fear and confusion. My hands tried their best to offer respite, but I couldn't reach her this time. How very sad that to celebrate the birth of the Prince of Peace so many exile themselves from the very kingdom he came to reveal . . .

Many bodywork practitioners are aware that from about mid-November through the end of each year, a different kind of energy presents itself on their table. Not only do regular clients tend to forgo their sessions in the rush of the "season," but even many of those who come are distracted by intensely conflicting emotions associated with family reunions, fulfilling the requirements of holiday traditions, and painful ambivalence toward our materialistic culture's way of celebrating.

Maintaining Our Own Inner Peace

As inner peace facilitators, there are numerous ways we can support, educate, and inspire others during this often difficult time of year. Number one, as always, is to maintain our own inner peace, no matter what! During this season especially, it is crucial that we be shining examples of embodied peace. When so many are being bombarded with lofty visions of Joy and spiritual sweetness that are often painfully at odds with their inner reality, there is a special need for healing artists to maintain a place where weary souls can reliably be touched by the true promise of the season, even if only for an hour or two.

As we consider the dis-ease so prevalent at this time of year, it may be useful for each of us to consider which of our behaviors contribute to being part of the *solution* and which add to the severity of the *problem*. For instance, by being especially attentive to our meditation or other spiritual practices, by avoiding overbooking our personal and professional lives, and by being especially vigilant in dealing with any inner conflicts we may be feeling in relation to this season's demands, we enhance our usefulness as servants of peace. Likewise, if we succumb to excessive eating, drinking, and partying, if we allow ourselves to become caught up in the rush and excitement—the excessive *doing* that surrounds us—our ability to be reliable, healing examples of the season's peace will be compromised, sometimes severely.

Expanding Awareness of Holiday Traditions

While monitoring our activities so that we maintain our inner balance, we might also carefully feed ourselves with the special spiritual food of this season. A tradition I practice is to contemplate the histories and realities that underlie our often frenzied and distorted outer celebrations. One basic reality, for those of us in the northern latitudes, is that the days are getting painfully short! The length of darkness has been growing daily for about five months now, and by December the heart is crying, "Enough!"

Many cultures at this time celebrate the return of light in some form. The Jewish Hanukkah commemorates the time when only a day's supply of oil for the sacred temple light miraculously lasted for eight. In Diwali, Hindus recall the return of their living light, Rama, after fourteen years of exile from his kingdom. Christmas, of course, celebrates the birth of Light, of the Prince of Peace, in human form. And Earth has her own special holy day at this time of year, the winter solstice, in which her cycle of tilting away from the Sun is completed and the process reverses, beginning a time of longer days and growing light.

Light Over Darkness

All of these sacred traditions in some way celebrate the victory of light over darkness, of spiritual truth over the darkness of ignorance. For those of us seeking to enact this victory within our own minds and hearts—and to help others to do likewise—this is a wonderful time to remember and appreciate the en-*light*-enment our work has released so far.

A major aspect of holiday time is the telling of stories. These include not only descriptions of the holidays themselves, but also all of the related personal stories in which we or our loved ones have been actors. Not only do such stories inform others of our traditions, but their retelling is often a cherished tradition all by itself.

Drawing upon this energy, you may find it useful to invite clients to recount some of the stories that underlie both the joy and trauma active for them in this season. In working with tales of pain, disappointment, or frustration, the focus can be on healing the old wounds through awareness, release of judgment and anger, and forgiveness.

Healing restores balance, an attribute increasingly absent during this season. One of my favorite reminders on this topic comes from Stephen Levine: "Balance arises when we enter, with mercy and aware-ness, areas that have been withdrawn from in fear and anger. Healing is a *rehabitation* of deserted areas of the mind-body, a living of our *whole* life." For inner peace facilitators, the holidays offer many challenging and rewarding opportunities to support and inspire our clients in their rehabitation process.

Encouraging Joy

In addition to facilitating healing work by airing and reframing painful personal stories, we might also invite the sharing of joyful mem-ories associated with this season. As the tellers become filled with the beauty and meaning of these special events, we can encourage them to make such activities more central in the current season and to be vigilant in avoiding the less-important distractions that confuse and draw precious energy away from what is most meaningful for them. While not sermonizing, we have a unique opportunity to reflect on how imbalance and not dealing effectively with inner conflicts are manifesting in chronic muscle tension. It can be gently pointed out that to the degree one is sincere in longing to experience the special peace of this season, vigilance in dealing with the causes of tension is imperative.

Especially at this time, I try to remember that my goal as an inner peace facilitator is to support the *expansion* of consciousness. A common tragedy of this season, though, is that its associated stress so often accomplishes exactly the opposite. If we are alert, we can find opportunities to help others reframe the meaning of what is happening in their lives. Getting in touch with what is truly meaningful during this unique time of year means *re-membering*—drawing back into awareness lost or confused "members" of inner consciousness. The energy of this season is also useful for intensifying commitments to melting the remaining inner obstacles that prevent ourselves and others from claiming our birthright, "the peace that passeth all understanding."

Celebrating Incarnation

When working with those for whom Christmas has meaning because it celebrates the incarnation of the Divine into flesh, it can be quite powerful to invite contemplation of this reality while massaging hands reflect into the recipients' consciousness the experience of *their own* state of incarnation. This might then lead to discussion of their own beliefs about the body-spirit relationship and how they feel about living in their body.

One way of understanding the Christmas story, especially when sharing it with children, is that this "birth day" of the Christ commemorates not only a historical event, but also the birth of Christ consciousness in each soul that invites it. Avoiding evangelical overtones, you may find it possible to suggest that it is receptivity—a willingness to accept more Consciousness, Love, and Truth in one's life—that is at the heart of this season. Advent, with its focus on anticipation of the transcendent joy to come, focuses on this aspect. Likewise, you may be able to encourage seekers of inner peace to draw from this season's energy to intensify their own longing for the clear, joyful revelation of spirit that is their destiny—the fulfillment of all their searching and inner transformation work.

Special Holiday Opportunities for Healing

A common pattern that many of us may observe in our clients (and ourselves!) is the attempt to recapture the good memories of childhood associated with this season and to avoid the painful, disappointed, and lonely feelings often triggered by the holiday's trappings. Yet as pilgrims traveling toward the birth of true peace, we are required to deal consciously with *everything* presented to us on our path—and especially the unpleasant arisings. Consciousness and Peace are synonymous; whatever distracts our awareness from our deepest truth, from the clarity required by our personal transformation work, eventually dilutes our inner peace.

So as the nearing holidays draw forth various emotions from our past, we can use this opportunity to intensify our own inner peacemaking efforts and to encourage those of similar mind to do likewise. The parts of us that are still children are particularly vulnerable at this time of year. Skilled, compassionate attention to their fears, needs, and longings can bring incredible joy and peace to one's inner family. And as our inner world is honored and finds harmony, its sweet song will naturally, subtly, and transformingly serenade our outer family, friends, and those we serve, inspiring them to deepen their quest for the true promise of this season of light.

One does not become enlightened
by imagining figures of light, but by
making the darkness conscious.

—*Carl Jung*

PART THREE

MORE DIALOGUES

The mind creates the abyss,
and the heart crosses it.
—*Stephen Levine*

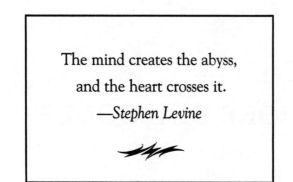

A "Technique" for Spiritual Inquiry

There is a wonderful line about healing work that I find both humbling and tremendously freeing:

> Technique is what we do to distract our
> clients while the real healing takes place.

In formal education everyone seems so obsessed about technique, about mastering the outer *forms* of the healing process. Yet as the discussion in this book has repeatedly asserted, true healing flows much more from who we *are* than from what we *do*. If we *are* peace—if personality's obstructions to the radiant, vibrant peace within have been made sufficiently transparent—this makes it easier for others around us who are ready to "come in tune." Our peace provides a natural safe haven for their work on themselves. And from our journey through disease, we've learned something of the nature of the path and so can offer useful guidance to those we encounter.

Since simply "being with" a wise person is not valued much in this culture, professionals usually employ some technique to project a feeling of legitimacy upon the client-practitioner encounter. And mastery of technique is definitely a useful tool! The problem is that practitioners can easily become seduced by their own projections of professional competence. Then, to use the analogy developed in chapter 10, they become lost in the darkened movie house of their personality, forgetting about the Sun, which is the original source of all they have to offer.

Inviting the Client's Higher Power

Having said this, let us now explore an approach to inner peace facilitation that can be a useful tool—or technique—for opening congested consciousness and nurturing the natural healing process. This involves inviting those we are helping to share their thoughts and feelings about a "higher power" in their life. What we are fishing for with this invitation are the spiritual principles that have already begun to cast their allure in this person's current stage of development. Since so many people have been abused and wounded by their religious upbringing, practitioners might avoid the word *God* until it becomes clear whether this is a negative (or even relevant) concept in the recipient's reality.

A large number of the clients I have seen have developed a meaningful connection with the Divine through one or more of the twelve-step programs. So I usually start by asking if there is a higher power operating in their life and see how they respond. The "technique" is then to adopt whatever terminology and spiritual beliefs they are comfortable with and reflect these back during the session to reinforce and expand their already existent understanding of Divinity. In addition to the Divine, useful "higher" helping agents might include angels, the spirit of a deceased loved one, or a favorite archetype of wisdom such as the "Wise Woman."

Since the supposed reason for us being together is massage, I also use this time to teach about the relationship between tension and suffering on the one hand and relaxation and expansion of consciousness on the other. By focusing on the dynamic of contraction and expansion as a primary principle affecting our lives, there are many opportunities to show how it applies and can be of use in the process of grappling with specific difficulties.

Focusing on Principles

As we talk, I find it useful to repeatedly "come back to basics." One of the first questions of the first session is, "Why have you come here today?" Usually the first round of answers involves things like tiredness, the desire to relax, specific pains or tensions, and, occasionally, a hunger for "something more" in life. Whatever is offered, I listen for hints of the issues that are already fermenting inside and offer encouragement to say more. This might reveal a desire for love (or a "relationship"), for freedom from an oppressive job situation, or for more joy in life.

A person being so questioned will almost always try to keep the focus on specific, safe "troubles" or wishes for something better. I counter this, then, with a reframing of whatever they offer in terms of higher *principles*. Then we can discuss together how these principles might be applied to help them get what they say they want.

The transformational power of such discussions, though, comes from the depth and thoroughness with which practitioners have already absorbed and integrated these principles into their own healing process. Revealing questions practitioners might work with include:

❖ What have I learned through my own experience that demonstrates the ability of principle-oriented dialogue to open and effectively deal with energetic blocks?

❖ In times of personal fear and vulnerability, how have I experienced the importance of a clear contract with a helping professional that sets and maintains appropriate boundaries to provide the emotional safety this process requires?

Out of our answers to such questions arises our ability to creatively incorporate dialogue and bodywork in a way that is useful and safe for the person we are supporting at the moment.

Frank's Dialogue with Karen

To see one way of how this approach might work, let us eavesdrop on a very abbreviated conversation as inner peace facilitator Frank talks with new client Karen. She has already said that she is writing a book and is frustrated because her creativity feels so blocked. Observing that Karen is sitting rather stiffly and sensing that some unconscious fear may be involved with her block, Frank initiates a dialogue intended to open up space for self-discovery and guide the bodywork that is to follow.

"So tell me, Karen," asks Frank, "what do you see as the source of your creativity? Does it come completely from within you, or is there something higher helping in this process?"

"Oh, I know it's not coming just from me. I don't like the word *God*, though. It makes me think of an old man with a white beard sitting in judgment."

Feminine Divinity?

"Perhaps you are more comfortable with a feminine form of Divinity," Frank suggests. "You know, whatever it was that created the universe is probably beyond any idea we have of masculine or feminine. Yet in order to deepen our relationship with this unimaginable creator, it's often helpful to give it a few human attributes. These are for our benefit, though, and in no way limit whatever Divinity actually is."

"Well, I'm definitely more comfortable thinking about the source of creation as feminine. Actually, I've become quite fascinated learning about the Goddess-worshiping religions recently."

After listening to Karen describe the thrill and peace she feels relating to the Divine as feminine, Frank invites her to call to the Goddess in her heart right now and seek her help in discovering and releasing the cause of her writer's block. They share a few moments of silence together, and when Karen speaks, her voice has a softer, more peaceful quality to it.

"You know, it's funny," she says, "how frightened I am of men. They can be so domineering sometimes!"

Remembering that Karen had spoken warmly of her brother earlier, Frank asks, "Does that include your brother also?"

"Oh, no," says Karen. "He's a sweetheart!"

Encouraging her to explore further, Frank asks, "How, then, is your brother's energy different from other men's?"

"Well, he listens and isn't always shoving his opinions at me."

"It sounds like you appreciate his feminine energy," Frank replies.

"Well, I hadn't thought about it in those terms, but, yes, when we're together his energy does help me get clearer about what I'm feeling."

Balancing Feminine and Masculine Qualities

Seeing an opportunity to include her writing block in the discussion, Frank asks, "Is it possible, Karen, that you have confused the essential qualities of masculine energy with the damaging and insensitive *use* of that energy by certain men in your life? It's just a thought, but perhaps what's keeping you from really getting into your writing project is a fear of *your own* masculine energy, of that part of you that knows what it wants and isn't afraid to move forward and get it. This assertiveness is part of each of us, though in cultures such as ours girls are taught to suppress it and think of it as unfeminine."

Karen takes a few moments to ponder this while Frank, who himself is quite comfortable praying to the Goddess, silently seeks her help in freeing Karen from unnecessarily constricted beliefs. Finally Karen says, "When I was younger, I was actually something of a tomboy; I did what I wanted and didn't much mind the teasing that came with it. But then, about fourteen, I became more interested in boys and changed. I think I lost something of myself as I tried to be popular, to fit in with my friends."

Bringing the conversation back to basic principles, Frank gently suggests that Karen did what she felt she had to do at that time in order to survive. But now the situation is different. She has much more experience and confidence, and perhaps she might be ready to release some of her older, unnecessarily limiting beliefs and habit patterns. Smiling, Frank wonders aloud, "What would have happened if the Goddess had blocked *her* assertive energy and never created the heavens and earth?"

Growing Relaxation from Inspiration

As Karen laughs, Frank notices how much more relaxed she is than when the session began less than an hour ago. While no physical touch has yet addressed her chronic muscle tension, their mutual willingness to allow Spirit (in this case, the Goddess) to inform and inspire their work has already brought forth many of the benefits that were expected from the bodywork. As they continue exploring together, Karen grows stronger in her understanding of how her negative judgments about masculine energy have prevented her from bringing forth the flower of her beautiful feminine intuition. Expanding her vision of the Goddess as integrating both masculine and feminine, Karen is now prepared to open herself in prayer differently.

As the talking part of the session comes to an end and they prepare to begin the hands-on work, Frank asks Karen to continue opening her masculine energy by focusing on her breathing during the massage. He suggests that she use her will to send each breath to the place being stretched at that moment and also that she continue to actively seek the Goddess's help in accepting and integrating whatever memories and emotions arise from the bodywork. He assures her that she is safe and can retain control even as she continues to soften her chronic defenses during the massage.

Creating Safety in Multiple Ways

In some inner peace facilitation sessions, by the time the hands-on work begins, the major part of that day's work has already been accomplished. The recipient may be noticeably more relaxed, energized, and ready to bring increased creativity and skill to whatever life is requiring. In such situations, the bodywork might be used as loving positive reinforcement, sort of like giving a lollipop to a child who has learned a lesson well. In other cases, what was begun in the talking part of the session continues tactilely, with the facilitator offering additional instruction and guidance in breathwork, sensory awakening, emotional awareness, and acceptance of any somatic memories that may come into consciousness.

The beauty of using an approach such as this is that it expands the healing process from just the limited physical-mental realm to include also the power and guidance of Spirit *in a way that feels safe to the client.* In psychology this is referred to as transpersonal work. If it were done within the context of a religion's dogma, it would be called pastoral counseling. But as client-centered inner peace facilitators, we don't use dogma to supply answers. We are neither experts nor authorities, but rather fellow seekers who, as humbly as possible, share with others what we are learning on our own inner journey. To the degree that we have developed mastery in *our* work, we are able to listen deeply and surrender our own "stuff" as we follow our inner guidance in supporting others in their quest for enduring peace.

It's vital to be growing through your life rather than going through your life. The object is not to change other people or situations; it's to do the inner work they stimulate.

—Wally Amos

The Tao Te Ching
and the Principle of Receptivity

The following client-practitioner dialogue is offered to convey a sense of how the Tao Te Ching *and the principle of receptivity might be integrated into inner peace counseling. A brief introduction to the* Tao Te Ching *is included at the end of this chapter.*

Ariel takes another sip of tea and considers how she'd like to begin her session today.

"I'm doing so much," she sighs, "and it's all *so* important! I keep trying to find ways to create more free time for myself, but it just isn't happening."

Listening, I sense a weariness in Ariel that is far more than just a need for a break. Something is clearly out of balance here; some inner wisdom is not being heard and followed. Feeling personally vulnerable to the same tendencies toward overinvolvement as Ariel has, I hesitate to advise.

> **To enter into the mystery where learning can occur, both desire and control must be relinquished. The desire to be right must give way to openness and receptivity to that which is.**

As these words from the book *Grace Unfolding: Psychotherapy in the Spirit of the Tao-te ching* by Greg Johanson and Ron Kurtz float through my mind, I can sense the intensity with which Ariel is clinging to both control and the need to be right. Perhaps there is something we can unfold together here that will help her feel safer in exploring the roots of this painful habit.

The Mystery Where Learning Can Occur

As a facilitator, a softness and deep compassion open inside me, poised delicately on a gentle willingness to be led into that "mystery where learning can occur." As if of their own accord, words flow and bridge the space between Ariel and myself.

"Ariel," I hear them saying, "I find your commitment to your work and the people you are serving so admirable! Yet at the same time I can feel the dis-ease, the chronic pain that you describe as part of this imbalance. Maybe we can open some space for regaining balance by playing in a different realm for a while."

With Ariel's consent, a foundation question is brought into our shared space: "What is the highest purpose in your life?" Unsure at first, Ariel gives answers that are vague. I encourage her to go deeper, to open to a level where her response evokes feeling, a sense of "Yeah, that's it!"

Ariel's Discovery

After a few tentative tries, Ariel's body shows a marked sense of relaxation as she smiles and says, "Well, I'm really here to learn how to love. I guess I've known that for a long time now, but I just haven't wanted to deal with all the stuff that's getting in the way."

> *Mindful, nonviolent therapy simply helps us discover and affirm the wisdom of our inner experience. . . . Therapists' work is more like that of a midwife.*

More thoughts from *Grace Unfolding* flow into my mind. I share a moment of stillness with Ariel as she experiences both sadness and joy in her realization that she has been using busyness as a shield to protect her from awareness of the deeper, perhaps painful, realities that are keeping her from fulfilling her heart's deepest longing.

When the words begin to flow once more, we continue exploring together some of these inner realities. Following her lead, I suggest additional ways of organizing her experiences, ways that might be more useful to her in fulfilling that growth for which her heart and spirit hunger. Later, as we continue this same exploration process in bodywork, Ariel feels bathed in safety and acceptance as she listens to the messages long hidden within her physical defense systems. Here, too, we seek new ways of understanding and organizing experience so that bound energy becomes available to support what is most important in her life.

Reminding People of Who They Have Always Been

In my life as a healing arts practitioner, I notice that my style and values are evolving beyond the more forceful, interventionist approach that drew me into this work originally. Ongoing "mentorship" training with a Taoist-trained professional supervisor and encounters with books such as *Grace Unfolding* are gradually persuading me of the value of *nondoing.* My can-do, activist mind, though, still has a hard time digesting the truths of this ancient path of wisdom and service:

> *Tao invariably takes no action, and yet there is nothing left undone. . . . Open yourself to the Tao, then trust your natural responses; and everything will fall into place. . . . The Sage only helps all creatures to find their own nature, but does not venture to lead them by the nose. . . . He simply reminds people of who they have always been.*

The practice of being in harmony with the Tao reminds me of the Buddhist practice of mindfulness. Both lead us along the path of wisdom by bringing the focus of our work back to ourselves, to the very processes in our minds that spin out our individual realities and the suffering that so often accompanies them. These and other wisdom traditions also assert that there is something more deeply real than our self-created models of reality. It may be called the Tao, our Buddha Nature, that which is revealed by the Holy Spirit in the temple of our soul, or other names depending upon the tradition and the understanding of the seeker.

Models of Reality

All of these wisdom traditions refer to a basic fact that I first encountered in a high school biology class. There we were taught that human beings filter out over 99 percent of all the sensory data that comes to us from outside. In addition, we often distort the data we do let in. Then, based on this highly selective information, we construct models of "reality" inside our minds about which we experience very real feelings that may have little to do with the original data. In most people, this model corresponds closely enough with what's actually "out there" that they are considered functional, even normal.

As inner peace facilitators, we enter into explorations with these "normal" people and help them learn to witness these self-constructed models of reality with a certain degree of detachment. In the Buddhist tradition, this is called "cultivating spaciousness"—that is, learning to see the products of the mind against a background of *nonmind.* The metaphor of observing bubbles arising in an ocean is used. Our thoughts, beliefs, and feelings are all bubbles, but usually we are so involved with the *content* of a particular bubble that we neglect to notice the surrounding ocean in which it arises, exists for a time, and dissolves. This exclusive identification with thoughts (bubbles) leads to a feeling of crampedness inside, a kind of spiritual claustrophobia from which we crave release, usually without even being able to name that spaciousness for which we hunger.

The Receptivity of Emptiness

In reading and seeking to absorb the wisdom in a book such as *Grace Unfolding,* I find myself both challenged and gently lifted out of the realm of confusion and conflicting beliefs into a clearer, simpler consciousness in which my heart and inner wisdom smile and murmur, "Yes, this is Truth, this is Home." One of the ways studying the Tao does this is by reminding me that what is truly most useful is the receptivity of my emptiness, *not* the amount of "learning" that both clutters up my mind and distracts me with pride and a false sense of competency.

Once more I find words from *Grace Unfolding* gently nourishing me:

> *Thirty spokes share the wheel's hub; it is the center hole that makes it useful. Shape clay into a vessel; it is the space within that makes it useful. Cut doors and windows for a room; it is the holes which make it useful. Therefore benefit comes from what is there; usefulness comes from what is not there.*

When in meditation or in times of peaceful reflection I contemplate my offerings as an inner peace facilitator, I notice how much I still desire to "help" others, to create for *myself* feelings of satisfaction and a belief that my life has meaning because I am an effective helper. As one who values the principles of client-centered therapy, I am forced to realize that I am not on track, that I have once more confused gratification of ego with that which is truly selfless service:

> *Ever desireless, one can see the mystery. Ever desiring,*
> *one sees the manifestations.*

Desireless Helpfulness

When client and therapist get bogged down in "stuff," in endless discussion of the minutiae of life and suffering, it is very difficult for healing to take place. To the degree that I play my role as facilitator out of a *desire* to be helpful, I see manifestations of problems, but rarely the source of them. To the degree that I enter a healing relationship *desire-less*, I am able to coexist both in the relationship of the moment *and* in the Great Mystery. This mystery contains this moment and also all moments, includes the confusions and fragmentations of now and also the clarity and wholeness of eternity. Desiring nothing, I can be an instrument of everything; wanting even to help, I become the helper and possess all his limitations.

> *. . . the Master acts without doing anything and teaches*
> *without saying anything. Things arise and she lets them come;*
> *things disappear and she lets them go.*

As my *mind* contemplates such thoughts, it becomes filled with questions and arguments. Yet when in stillness such wisdom percolates into the deeper reaches of my being, I find a smile creeping onto my face and a gentle awareness of Truth, of the mystery, in which healing takes place.

Deepening the Feminine

Recently, such contemplations have led me toward an increasing awareness of the deeply feminine nature of this approach. When identifying with the mind and its penetrating, active nature, we are in a masculine mode of being. But when we become receptive, aware, seeking only to maintain and deepen our own balance as consciousness expands to embrace more and more of the Great Mystery, then it is the feminine that leads.

Since most of us find ourselves living in a culture that values and magnifies the importance of masculine approaches, it may be useful to intentionally practice ways of being that develop and nurture our feminine sides. Meditation, contemplation, prayer, peacefully being in nature, great art, willing vulnerability in relationships—all of these provide useful counterbalances to the excessively masculine energies most of us find demanded of us in the activities of our normal lives.

Another approach toward developing the feminine is to pay more attention to the language we use to describe our inner realities, both to others and to ourselves. A famous anthropologist, Benjamin Whorf, hypothesized that we each experience reality through the structure of the language in which we think. The Hopi language, for instance, has no way to distinguish past, present, and future, so for the Hopi, time is a continuous *now*. As one whose linguistic ability is limited to English, I find it almost impossible to experience the nature of such a reality, although through mental approximations I've come to believe that it may well represent a much more accurate description of Reality.

Language and Reality

Likewise, there is an inherent masculine bias in the structure of the English language that makes it quite difficult to describe inner states of being. The basic structure is active: I (subject) want (verb) the book (object). In creating sentences, we automatically fall into a pattern in which a subject "verbs" or does something, manipulates something, uses will to cause something to happen. In order to describe feminine states of being, we are forced by our language to use the pseudo verbs such as *be* (I am thoughtful) or *feel* (She feels puzzled). By structurally linking subject and state of being as if the latter were an object, we're left with a subtle confusion between being and doing. And then, to make matters even worse, most of us were taught in school that writing in the passive (feminine, receptive) voice is weak and should be avoided.

With the very structure of the language in which we perceive life and the "rules" we are taught for using it so heavily focused on masculine approaches, it is no wonder that we experience frustration as we attempt to open ourselves (become femininely receptive) to the Great Mystery. That is why books such as *Grace Unfolding* and Ram Dass and Paul Gorman's *How Can I Help?* as well as Stephen Levine's books and tapes are so very useful in our quest for greater receptivity. By skillfully using words to dance meaning into inherently unexplainable truths, these authors demonstrate ways of dancing meaning into our own realities. Their examples show how we can use words (and the masculine mind that projects them) to express and share that which is deeply feminine.

Harmonizing Feminine and Masculine

Ariel rests for awhile after her bodywork and then shares some of her observations from the session.

"I had never realized," she says, "that the continuous drive to always be *doing* more is really my masculine energy out of balance with my inner feminine. I can see now that harmonizing these two principles is really my need, not using one to control the other. I want to experience Grace unfolding inside me also, and I think I now have some better ways of working with those habit patterns that interfere with the free flow of this Grace. I'm going to be much more protective of my receptive feminine side, and I suspect that's going to bring me a lot more of the peace I've experienced here today."

One final bit of wisdom from the *Tao Te Ching* is shared:

> **Be content with what you have; rejoice in the way things are. When you realize there is nothing lacking, the whole world belongs to you.**

We both smile and enjoy a last few moments of silence together.

About the Tao-Te Ching

Excerpts from the introduction to the book *Grace Unfolding: Psychotherapy in the Spirit of the Tao-te ching.*

I *have found* Grace Unfolding *by Gregory J. Johanson and Ronald S. Kurtz to be an extraordinarily useful book for deepening understanding of the principles of inner peace facilitation. Written in delightful, nontechnical language, this book serves two purposes: it illuminates basic principles of noninvasive therapeutic counseling and also provides excellent guidance for inner peace facilitators in evaluating and choosing a personal therapist, mentor, and/or professional supervisor. Following are excerpts from the introduction to the book.*

Sometime during the sixth to fourth centuries B.C. the mysterious Lao Tzu bequeathed us the *Tao-te ching,* a book which would become the foundational text of the spiritual/philosophical school of Chinese thought called Taoism. . . . Although more than one hundred translations of Lao Tzu's work have been made, it has generally retained its Chinese title, *Tao-te ching.* In English this might be rendered as "The Classic (*ching*) of the Way (*Tao*) and Its Virtue (*te*)."

The *Tao-te ching* is a mystical or spiritual book because it presents the Tao, or the Way, as the source, truth, or creative principle behind all appearances of life. Like God in the Western tradition, the Tao can never be captured in words. A practical, philosophical training manual, the *Tao-te ching* encourages us to embody virtue, to live lives that are consistent with the reality of the Tao. With poetic grace it seeks to help us bring our being and our doing into harmonious unity.

Lao Tzu's teachings were written during a time when old structures were declining. Trade and business were growing with the advent of new technologies. Rulers flaunted their power, developed new weapons systems, and called for law and order to quiet the restless masses. Confucianism, the philosophy of the day, emphasized the values of conformity and worldly treasure. Life was both busy and unhappy.

Into this volatile and complex situation that seemingly called for much to be done, Lao Tzu introduced the ideas of nonbeing, nondoing, and nonviolence. Nonbeing was a revolutionary concept for the

Chinese. It has also been a difficult concept for Westerners because it does not mean "nothing" or "emptiness" as the Greeks and those that followed them understood it. For Lao Tzu, nonbeing is the foundation of being, more like "everything" than it is like "nothing." Like the hub of a wheel or the hollow of a cup, it is the empty space that makes things useful. Nonbeing gives being the space to exist. An analogous thought is found in an ancient Jewish myth that says in the beginning God was everything, so the only way God could create was by withdrawing, disappearing, to allow the space for life to emerge. Nonbeing suggests not identifying with part of anything, or of ourselves, but embracing all, excluding nothing. Similarly, nondoing for Lao Tzu does not mean doing nothing, but rather not interfering, doing only those things which are natural and in line with the movement of our ever-changing world.

Nonbeing and nondoing were such radical notions that no one knew what to make of them. . . . Still, the unmistakable rightness of Lao Tzu's teaching was intuitively recognized. It became a powerful though subtle underground influence, continuing through the centuries until the present. Lao Tzu pointed to the simple and unforced, to a gentle influence rather than effort or struggle. For him, nondoing was not a way to withdraw from involvement with life, but rather a way to achieve realization in life through actively and consciously maintaining harmony with the Way Things Are.

Together, nonbeing and nondoing support nonviolence. Nonviolence is an attitude of trust in creation, especially the natural changes which flow from the interaction of being and nonbeing. It is a commitment to not interfere with the processes of life, but to celebrate their spontaneous, organic intelligence. Nonviolence promotes a respect for the subtle, almost imperceptible movements of mind, body, and spirit, and gives rise to a yielding or softness which follows and nourishes these movements rather than correcting or conquering them.

Obstacles are what you see when you
take your eyes off the goal.
—*Wally Amos*

SIXTEEN

The Times, They Are A-Changin'

In addition to exploring how inner peace facilitation can be helpful to clients, we might also consider how insightful dialogue and sharing wisdom teachings can be supportive and nourishing between practitioners and friends. The following is offered to demonstrate such sharing.

On a lovely spring day, Chris and Carolyn are enjoying lunch on Carolyn's patio, bathed in the brilliant green of new growth and the heart-stirring song of returning birds. Both are experienced massage practitioners, and they often meet to share the trials and delights of their profession. In recent years, Chris has been incorporating the principles of inner peace facilitation into the ongoing transformational focus of her practice. Carolyn, while still quite traditional, is curious about her friend's growing delight in this new approach to her work.

The Deeper Meaning of Healing

One topic that these colleagues often discuss is the deeper meaning of healing. Both are committed to alleviating the suffering of their clients, but increasingly Chris is drawn to seek change at deeper levels, both in herself and in those she serves. As their conversation evolves, Carolyn shares some of the despair she is feeling over the suffering she sees increasing everywhere and her inability to make any sense of what's happening. Chris, ever the healer ready to explore, shares some of what she's been learning lately.

"Ever hear of 'eco-psychology'?" asks Chris as Carolyn serves their dessert. A puzzled look prompts Chris to explain. "Just as the science of biological ecology seeks to understand behavior in the context of larger systems, eco-psychology asserts that human thoughts, feelings, and inner models of reality are inevitably interrelated with the social and physical environments in which they exist.

"As an inner peace facilitator, I'm learning to act as a guide for clients wishing to explore the nature of their inner reality. In a sense, I act as 'system-integration consultant,' showing clients how thought systems, feeling systems, and body systems are all interconnected. As I help explore how unresolved childhood trauma can feed current patterns of physical and emotional pain, and as I support clients in directly experiencing these inner realities, I often also uncover pain and woundedness arising out of the 'dis-ease' of the physical and social world around us."

Our Response to Tension

Carolyn nods, glad for her friend's help in understanding more deeply many of her own observations over the years.

"Just consider," Chris continues, "how often you have massaged clients' knotted neck and shoulder muscles while hearing stories of people and situations in their lives that are a 'pain in the neck.' Ever turn on the news out of a sense of relaxed curiosity and ten minutes later feel yourself in pain? Some of us are so empathetic that we inwardly experience the suffering of others. Sometimes, too, the enormity of the world's problems weigh heavy upon our shoulders, and we find ourselves contracting unconsciously against the overwhelming feelings associated with this awareness.

"If I think of myself primarily as an activist, I'll tend to respond to information about outer suffering by *doing* something to change conditions *out there.* If I am more influenced by the orientation of traditional psychotherapy, I'll tend to focus more on inner *adjustment,* on individuals *changing their responses* to inner and outer experiences. Each of these are vital and necessary responses to the conditions we experience in our lives, and I'm finding that skillful integration of *both* goes a long way toward creating healthier lives for myself and my clients."

After pausing to let Carolyn digest these ideas—and to have another helping of dessert herself—Chris elaborates further. "You know how much we've talked about inner peace and how hard it is to sustain it.

What I'm gradually coming to realize, Carolyn, is that while inner psychological adjustment and outer involvement in change are both important, something more must be added. I've seen it called by various names: the transpersonal, living according to God's will, the principled life, dharma, and heeding the still, small voice within are just a few terms that refer to it. Sometimes when we've talked, I've called it the vertical element, that which takes us up beyond our human consciousness and is the focus of our heart's deepest longing and aspiration. However we understand it, this third 'point' is essential for balance."

Adding the Third Leg

"Here's an example I sometimes share with my clients," Chris goes on. "If you are trying to sit on a two-legged stool, you must always be alert to falling either forward or backward. It is an inherently unstable situation, though the 'freedom' to rock back and forth can be exhilarating at times. Add a third leg, however, and your 'seat' is stable on any surface, no matter how uneven or bumpy. This is a tripod, and of all possible combinations of 'legs,' it is the only one that finds stability on *any* surface.

"Likewise, most of the time we are operating as if we were two-legged stools. One leg is 'me' and the second is 'other.' It really doesn't matter what 'other' is: my boss, lover, children, environment, or society. When there's just subject and object in our consciousness, we are in an inherently unstable situation. A little investigation shows why.

"Just as in a sentence, the subjects and the objects in our lives are always connected by a verb, by an action that arises out of some motivation such as desire, fear, attraction, repulsion, or longing. As we've discussed so often, much of the time we experience conflicting motivations. How, then, does this inner conflict evolve into an outer action? This question alone is a wonderful focal point for inner peace explorations!

"As we get more familiar with our inner processes, we discover patterns of behavior with roots in past trauma. We find that these patterns reflect conflicting values, and if we look carefully, we may notice ourselves spending endless hours trying to 'solve' these conflicts while rocking on our inner two-legged stool of 'me' and 'my desires.' We *try* so hard, yet seem to make so little lasting progress!

"This is why the transpersonal 'third leg' is so very important. By bringing something greater than 'me' into our deliberations, we introduce a stabilizing factor, a source of guidance that, if followed, draws forth the serenity and joy we so long for."

Carolyn reflects quietly for a while. "This reminds me," she says, "of our talk last month. I remember your telling me how you guide clients in investigating the process by which our perceptions are formed into inner models of what we consider to be reality and how we then confuse these models with Reality itself."

Modeling Reality

"That's right," says Chris, smiling. "So much of my work now deals with exploring how we *organize* our experiences and perceptions. When we change our inner organization, our sense of what's real changes also. Do we understand our experiences and express ourselves through a lens of fearful, distorting illusions and end up harming ourselves and others? Or do we more accurately perceive our interdependence with all life and, in this awareness, live with compassion and gratitude for what we experience both inside and out?"

"Oh boy," sighs Carolyn, "this links back to our discussions of epistemology—of how we know what we know and how we discern between the greater truth and the lesser one in situations of conflict."

Delighted that their thoughts are so harmonious, Chris grins and exclaims, "That's it! And working with this fundamental question, perhaps we can more clearly understand the changes occurring everywhere and see how we're called to participate."

From One Era to the Next

Carolyn looks puzzled, so Chris explains her thinking more fully. "We've all heard that we are at the end of one era on this planet and coming into another. In astrology it's called the end of the Piscean age and the beginning of the Aquarian age. In the thought system of India, we are now at the end of Kali Yuga, the 'iron age'—the lowest, or most crude, of the ages of human consciousness. Another translation of Kali Yuga is 'machine age,' a time when the machinelike nature of humans is valued more highly than our other attributes.

"Now, machines are great for *doing* things. But for centuries the masculine value of 'doing' has been emphasized so much that we've almost lost our connection with that part of ourselves that knows *what's worth doing*. That's the feminine side, the receptive, the inner center where experience is distilled into wisdom. A certain quietude is generally required, though, to 'hear' the wisdom of this inner center, since it is subtler than the messages screaming at us from our egos.

"So maybe," Chris continues, "the change we are sensing around us is the pendulum swinging back from its 'doing' extreme, slowly returning to a center that more highly values wisdom and the inner peace necessary for its growth. As this center opens in us, we become able to work more skillfully with the questions that, in the maturity of wisdom, naturally precede doing. What is the other person's 'stuff,' and what is my own? What is the greater truth of this moment? What am I called on to 'do' in this moment? Does this action maintain harmony and serve my highest values?"

"Whew!" exclaims Carolyn. "You make it sound as if the coming age will be one never-ending philosophy class!"

"Actually, if we're lucky, it will be more like an ongoing meditation session," replies Chris with a twinkle in her eyes. "We're using all these words now because we're so used to *thinking* about everything. But as our receptive, sensing, feeling parts develop, perhaps our lives will be more like a lovely dance in which our every 'doing' is in step with the 'music' of Love and the rhythm of Truth."

"That's a beautiful vision, Chris, but how do we get from here to there? Does it just happen by itself as the ages change? Or can we consciously participate in some way?"

The Meaning of Virtue

The two friends are quiet for a moment, pondering the vast rhythms of life. Then Chris says, "Both, Carolyn. What fascinates me, though, is discovering my own unique role in this unfolding play. Since I'm drawn to thinking about the nature of wisdom and peace, my work seems to be creating an inner environment that is conducive for these investigations. And you know what I'm discovering? The common social virtues that most of us were taught as children have meaning much deeper than I had ever guessed. They are fundamental in spiritual traditions all over the world—fundamental in the sense of *necessary as an inner condition for expanding our consciousness,* our ability to directly perceive what's what. So now when I explore my inner patterns or work with a client, I look for connections between pain-producing behavior on the surface and disregard for fundamental virtues underneath. And it's amazing what a clear link there is!"

"It's interesting that you're mentioning this," muses Carolyn. "The word *purity* has been haunting me lately. I was reading an article in a spiritual magazine about how they make the silicon chips that power computers. Evidently, one particle of dust can ruin a thousand-dollar chip, so they spend a huge amount of money creating 'clean rooms,' and workers are required to wear special clothing to minimize the introduction of any impurities. Then it went on to say that our consciousness is like one of those chips and requires great inner purity to function properly. Yet most of us spend very little on creating a 'clean room' inside, a place where our awareness and ability to process information in wisdom and peace can operate without the destructive dust of mental agitation, cravings, and fear."

Gently, Chris nods her head in agreement. "All those virtues I spent so much time rebelling from in my childhood were nothing other than instructions for creating that inner 'clean room.' Now I'm relearning them, but in a very different context. I don't need to be kind to others to please Mommy and Daddy any more—I do it because to act unkindly disturbs my inner peace and interferes with accessing the wisdom I need to joyfully live, work, and grow. And I seek to act and speak truthfully not so much out of fear of being caught, but because to do otherwise wastes a whole lot of energy and creates enmeshment in 'stories' that create confusion and disturb my peace."

After a few moments for reflection, Carolyn wonders out loud, "This inner work must take a lot of time and energy from your life. Don't you worry about not spending more time learning new techniques for your work? Doesn't it sometimes feel a bit selfish being so focused on yourself?"

Allying with the Light Forces

Chris was thoughtful. "I wonder about the questions you've raised also," she says. "But I also wonder about the changes I see all around me—about the increase of destruction and suffering, and about the rising forces of something light, wonderful, and balanced. I want very much to be an ally of these new light forces and to help others learn about them also.

"I had an interesting experience last month. You remember my telling you about the workshop for massage practitioners I taught in Michigan? Well, at the end, when I read the comments on the evaluation forms, almost all of the participants said that even though the techniques and information they had learned were valuable, the most important part was the spiritual aspect of the work—the explicit inclusion of a higher power into the inner peace counseling and the bodywork. Now, Carolyn, doesn't being a conduit for this higher power mean developing virtue? Isn't the best investment in my career spending the time and energy necessary to learn about how I work inside and seeking to attune these processes more harmoniously with what I value most?

"So often after a session a client will ask what technique I used, and I never know how to answer. If I were to be honest, I'd have to say that my 'technique' is practicing getting out of the way and letting God work through me. But that is so easily misunderstood, so I sometimes use the metaphor of a midwife. To the degree a client is ready, is 'pregnant' with balance and health wanting to emerge, my work is to come in tune with this process—to push or pull in ways that support what's ready to happen anyway. There's a lot of listening involved—such a need for the feminine 'virtue' of receptivity. The 'doing' then arises very naturally. Techniques—when called for—are a spontaneous outgrowth of this attunement."

A Curriculum for the Times to Come

"Boy," sighs Carolyn, "what you're talking about sure doesn't sound anything like what I learned in massage school!"

"Perhaps not," agrees Chris, "but it may be the beginning of a curriculum that prepares us for the times to come. There's so much wisdom available to us! Bodies will teach us if we are willing to listen and accept their messages. Higher powers abound that will utilize whatever we make available to the healing process. And this process is always circular: the healing we think we are sharing with others comes back to enrich and nurture our own inner realm, softening and giving meaning to the birth pangs of new awareness that illuminates our many dark corners."

"I'm so glad we can talk together like this," says Carolyn. "You give voice to thoughts I haven't known how to express. Just hearing my inner truth spoken out loud increases my understanding and commitment so much—it's like my heart is receiving a warm, loving massage!"

With a twinkle in her eye, Chris says, "I like the way one of my favorite teachers, Ram Dass, puts it: 'I'm not telling you anything you don't already know—I'm just your rent-a-mouth.'" Smiling, the two friends sit together silently and enjoy the peace of their communion.

Your pain is the breaking of the shell
that encloses your understanding.
—*Kahlil Gibran*

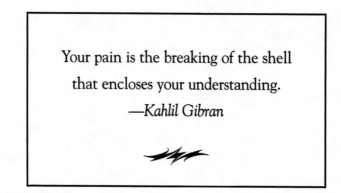

SEVENTEEN

Yoga and Freedom

It has been more than a month since Chris and Carolyn last visited. Carolyn, still under the influence of their conversation in the previous chapter, has begun hatha yoga lessons and is continuing her fledgling meditation practice. Enjoying the warmth of their deepening friendship—and of a sumptuous lunch—the two colleagues have been exploring the "big questions" again . . .

A butterfly flitters across the patio table and gently lands on the edge of Carolyn's melon. Entranced, the women stop speaking and watch in silence as shimmering wings reflect the noonday sun. Dazzling color filling their consciousness, each is one with this living beauty and freedom.

The moment ends as wings once more engage in flight, but a tender silence still holds Chris and Carolyn. After a time speech returns, and they continue their conversation.

"I wish I could be that free," muses Carolyn.

"Well, you can," laughs Chris, a mischievous smile on her face. "Just keep on meditating, doing your yoga, getting bodywork . . ."

Still somewhat skeptical, Carolyn finds it difficult to share Chris's faith that she will ever know the butterfly's freedom. "Listen, Chris," she replies, "I accept that I need to broaden the repertoire of skills that I can share with my clients, but even the best massage I ever received didn't leave me light enough to fly!"

"How sad," pouts Chris in mock sympathy. "Maybe a little more practice . . ."

A recurring theme with these friends has been the need to continually attend to their own inner development in order to deepen their ability to be a valuable healing resource for their clients. Aware that they are often asked professionally for guidance in areas far removed from their original training, these colleagues have been intensively deepening their awareness and abilities in numerous fields. Recently, hatha yoga has become a shared interest, with Chris's broader understanding illuminating Carolyn's new experiences.

Massage as Two-Person Yoga

"One of the ways I describe my bodywork," continues Chris, "is that it's like a form of two-person yoga. You know how when you relax into a yoga posture, gravity helps you deepen the stretch. We're taught that with each out-breath we're to let go a little further into the posture, focus our awareness on the nature of the resistance, and discover how to release a little more of whatever tension is keeping us from fully manifesting that particular form.

"In my massage work, the process is the same, only my hands—not gravity—provide the stretching force. When we're really working together for transformation, though, the client is engaged just like in hatha yoga: breathing deeply, releasing tension on the out-breath, and dealing with any emotional 'stuff' that this process may be bringing to the surface."

"Are you saying," asks Carolyn, "that when this process has evolved far enough, I'll feel as free as that butterfly?"

"Even freer!" says Chris in all seriousness. "The butterfly's freedom is instinctive, is limited by its nature. For us also, our freedom is limited by our nature—by our genetic programming, personal habits, and social conditioning. But as humans, we have the potential to transcend our nature. We can choose to evolve into something more, just as the beauty and freedom of that butterfly evolved out of a land-bound, dull-green caterpillar."

"Sounds like we're getting back into that spiritual stuff again," quips Carolyn.

Yoga Means Union

"Well, of course," responds Chris, "the term *spiritual* is just another way of referring to our innate longing and ability to evolve, to transform. You may have heard that the Sanskrit word *yoga* actually means 'union,' as in union with God. In the Eastern traditions, it is commonly understood that each human begins as a spark of divinity, then becomes identified with a human body through many lifetimes, and eventually remembers, reidentifies with that All-ness of which it has always been a part. The condition of thinking we are *only* a human is called *ignorance*. In this state, we remember almost none of our innate spiritual freedom, and hence we suffer.

"More and more," Chris continues, "I find myself spending extra time with interested clients discussing their spiritual background and current beliefs, encouraging them to go more deeply into whatever spiritual practices make sense to them, to remember that we are ever so much more than this misery-prone body we take so seriously. We work with the body, honor and respect its needs and wisdom, but if we stop there, we'll never fly!

"Because I know that all spiritual traditions are able to support transformation and help us remember our true nature, I find myself as a healer working with whatever belief systems my client holds dear. As in other areas of our lives, most of us have conflicting spiritual beliefs. The physical tension produced by these chronic conflicts is a large part of what we attempt to free up with our massage. As these long-standing conflicts begin to resolve, we can explore our inner realm more deeply. And when we fearlessly investigate, I'll bet most of us find that it is *not putting into practice* our spiritual beliefs that gets us into trouble, not the beliefs themselves."

"This reminds me of our discussion last month of virtue and its role in developing the inner purity necessary for genuine spiritual unfolding," adds Carolyn.

Virtue and Purity

"How true," says Chris. "Terms like *virtue* and *purity* sound antiquated and almost odd these days, but in every spiritual tradition they are understood to be prerequisites for advanced development. If we look at the matter objectively, it's pretty easy to understand why.

"The opposite of virtue is any thought, word, or deed that makes us heavy, that moves our state of being or vibrations out of harmony with Truth, dharma, or God's will. Likewise, virtue refers to whatever brings our inner reality in tune with the greater reality. Since Reality is inherently joyful and light, harmonizing our thoughts and actions with it engenders these same feelings in us also. It's interesting that in hatha yoga, the various postures are designed to promote certain virtues, activating the subtle centers where each virtue resides.

"The old saying 'Virtue is its own reward' is based on a deep realization of the nature of spiritual mechanics. Another saying that refers to the same truth is, 'Angels can fly because they take themselves lightly.'

"Another way of thinking of virtue is that which nurtures the unfolding of our angelic nature, fulfilling the longing you feel to be as free as a butterfly. Virtue makes us light, relaxed, and peaceful; it prepares us for actually realizing—not just dreaming about—our heart's deepest longing. And to the degree that we assist our clients in linking the lightness and peace they experience as a result of our massage with inner patterns that maintain that freedom, then we are truly offering healing and transformative education."

Patanjali's Eight-Step Path to Freedom

"It's humbling to realize that thousands of years ago great spiritual teachers described in precise detail this enlightenment process," Chris elaborates. "One of these great ones, Patanjali, lived in India and described an eight-step journey to complete freedom. In the first two steps of this self-mastery process ten moral principles—or virtues—are described. And you know what's interesting? These ten are almost identical to the ten commandments in our Western tradition."

"You mean like don't kill or steal?" asks Carolyn.

"Of course those are included," replies Chris, "but there are subtler aspects of each that most of us rarely consider. For instance, the Sanskrit word *ahimsa,* which Gandhi made famous, means nonviolence. While this includes not doing physical harm to anyone, including yourself, it has a deeper meaning also. On this subtle level, *ahimsa* refers to avoiding violent thoughts, to being vigilant and dissolving feelings of disrespect, anger, or blame before they become rooted in the mind or express themselves outwardly. One could easily spend a lifetime mastering this one virtue!

"Nonlying, in its subtler meaning, refers to awareness of various levels of truth and an ongoing commitment to honoring the greater truths over lesser ones. Nonstealing in its subtler understanding means not desiring anything that is not yours. Nongreed means not being attached even to what is rightfully yours. And nonsensuality, which is sometimes understood to mean celibacy, really refers to a much deeper nonattachment to bodily sensations."

"I see how these all fit together to make our consciousness lighter," muses Carolyn, "yet isn't there a contradiction in a bodyworker counseling nonsensuality? Don't we encourage our clients to be *more* sensually aware?"

Chronic Tension and Attachment

"I can see where that might be confusing," Chris responds. "Remember, though, each of these principles is designed to free us from *attachment*. To do this, we often need to be much more *aware* of just how deep our habits of clinging really are. Nonsensuality in the yogic sense is quite different from being dissociated from bodily realities such as chronic tissue constriction, which hides awareness of traumatic memory.

"I think it's important to help our clients understand that tension itself is a natural and necessary part of life; it's only when we can't *let go,* when the tension becomes *chronic,* that we crave release on the table. Likewise, sensual awareness is necessary for both survival and enjoyment of life. But when we become *attached* to any particular sensual experience, be it the tang of a fine salsa or our lover's embrace, our degree of attachment defines our loss of freedom. When attachment is associated with certain chemicals, we call it addiction and accept it as a problem. But attachment or addiction itself—even to apparently healthy experiences—is the real culprit. *Any* attachment keeps us from our destiny, which is to fly free."

Carolyn reflects quietly for a few moments, soberly reviewing the various attachments in her life, noticing how each limits her inner freedom. As she explores several of them, she notices the inherent tension associated with each. Then looking up at the blue sky, she feels the tension releasing. In its place is a sweet longing to be free of *any* bondage, to be light enough to play with the butterfly and discover for herself the land of the angels. When Carolyn's gaze returns to Chris, she seems refreshed, ready to learn more about this ancient path that leads to freedom from all attachments.

Forward on an Ancient Path

"There's a certain irony here," adds Chris. "Many of us seek enlightenment in order to *transcend* our limited personality, or ego. But as our development of these fundamental virtues reveals their subtler levels and opens our awareness, we are forced to confront the weaknesses of our ego and deal with them!

"These, incidentally, are the root of chronic defense systems such as muscle armoring. As we grow stronger in this process of spiritual growth, though, such habitually defensive stances toward life are no longer necessary. Eventually an ego becomes mature. Then it's like fruit on a tree: when it's 'ripe,' it just naturally and easily 'lets go.' Until then, though, pulling on it risks damaging the tree.

"Although students of the eight-step path might spend 90 percent of their time just becoming reasonably proficient in the basic virtues, these comprise only the first two steps," continues Chris. "The third is called *asana*, or what we refer to as yoga postures. These are scientific procedures for releasing bound tension and developing suppleness and steadiness both in our physical and subtle bodies. Hatha yoga classes are a great way to get started, but they can go only as deep as the development of the particular teacher allows.

"The fourth step is called *pranayama*, or breath control. In the ancient science of India, breath and energy are understood to be the same thing. So controlling *prana* means not only utilizing specific breathing exercises, but also becoming proficient in guiding the movement of energy on all inner levels. Then comes *pratyahara*, or the interiorization of mind. This focuses one's consciousness so that the thoughts don't wander in endless restlessness and delusion."

"Heavens!" exclaims Carolyn, "I'm sure if I could do that I would already be quite enlightened."

"So it may seem to us now," replies Chris, "but according to those who've completed the process, there are still three more levels to go. The sixth is called *dharna*, which means fixing awareness on a single idea or object. If one has had the good fortune to experience a glimpse of divinity at some point in life, this memory might provide such a focal point. Others can simply bring all their attention to that which their heart holds most dear."

The Culmination of Meditation

"It is only then, after these first six stages are mastered, that true meditation, or *dhyana*, is possible," Chris concludes. "In the scientific sense of this process, meditation refers to becoming one with that for which we long most deeply. If we could truly meditate on perfect peace, our very nature would be transformed into peace. Finally, the culminating stage is called *samadhi*, enlightenment, oneness with God."

There being nothing more to say, the two friends relax in the joy of the path they feel opening before them. While each experiences delight in considering her own eventual enlightenment, thoughts also arise of how they can share these principles with clients who hunger for greater freedom and who are ready to take their next step on the road Home.

Much of the information in this chapter comes from a booklet entitled "The Paths of Yoga" *by Sri Kriyananda (see resources in chapter 21).*

We have to go down and in, and on
the way we meet monsters. But if we
ride those monsters all the way
down, we find the most precious
thing of all: the unified field, our
complex and inexplicable caring for
one another, the community we
have underneath our brokenness,
our life together. . . . Great leadership comes from people who have
made that downward journey.
—*Parker J. Palmer*

Healing the Wounds that Bind

The following client-practitioner dialogue illustrates further the inner child work introduced earlier. It describes the technique of creating a time bridge between the adult and the wounded child and introducing a loving presence to facilitate that child's healing.

Sharon is happy as her client Jason follows her into the interview room. This is Jason's third facilitating inner peace session, and judging from the enthusiasm and commitment he's demonstrated so far, she anticipates being able to utilize her spiritual midwifery skills to their fullest today. After sharing a cup of tea and catching up on recent happenings in Jason's life, Sharon gently steers the discussion into deeper—and perhaps riskier—areas.

"Last week," she begins, "I remember your description of the period in your life when drinking was such a problem. And I was so impressed hearing how you came out of it with the help of Alcoholics Anonymous. Even though alcohol is not my own particular addiction, I could really identify with some of the underlying patterns."

Alcoholism and Recovery

"I had a feeling that you could empathize with what I was saying," replies Jason. "It was a long, painful struggle, and it's far from over."

Sharon looks puzzled and asks, "Please excuse my confusion, but didn't you tell me you've been sober for the last seven years?"

"That's right," confirms Jason, "but one of the teachings in AA is that your recovery goes on long after you stop drinking. Once we begin to understand the underlying patterns that fed our drinking, we realize that we are always vulnerable to their influence and hence must keep growing in our recovery. There's a saying in AA that you're either going forward or going backward in your recovery—there's no standing still."

"This is also a general truth in many spiritual traditions," adds Sharon. Smiling, she says to Jason, "I'm looking forward to learning more about your recovery process and how AA's approach helped you—I think it will help me better understand several other clients also."

After a pause, Sharon continues. "Perhaps you could share with me some of what you experienced in our last session that has helped you move forward."

Jason's face lights up, and he answers almost immediately. "Well, the work you did during the massage on my gluteal muscles was a real eye-opener. I've had lots of work in that area from other practitioners, but I never experienced work that deep or felt the emotions stored there before."

Repressed Rage and Sorrow

Waiting while he collects his thoughts, Sharon smiles encouragingly for him to continue. "What was so amazing," volunteers Jason, "was how strongly I could feel the wounded little boy inside. I told you about how my dad used to beat me when I was a kid, but until last week my awareness of the pain was all in my head. I had no idea that I had stored so much repressed rage and sorrow in my body—especially in my butt, of all places."

Sharon grins and adds, "Well, it's a secret with hints built right into our language. Don't we acknowledge that when we have a problem too big to handle at the moment, we 'sit on it'? And when someone is really bothering us, don't we refer to that person as a 'pain in the ass'?

"Storage of repressed pain in this area is so prevalent that even though most of my clients come in asking for work in their neck and shoulders, I know that for deeper, long-term release, a lot of gluteal work will be necessary also. When the muscles in the pelvic area are chronically in spasm, it makes it very difficult for the spine to be supported properly at its base. When that's pulled out of balance, the whole body system has to compensate in ways that leave the neck and shoulders out of balance. I've learned that I can massage the upper body till

I'm blue, but if there isn't corresponding work in the pelvic area, the relaxation won't hold for long.

"There's a kind of work called 'structural integration,' or 'rolfing,' in which practitioners use an even more comprehensive approach and start with the feet, gradually establishing balance from contact with the ground up. So many times I've gone for a rolfing session complaining of neck pain and watched as the practitioner spent 90 percent of the time on my feet and legs. But then the last few minutes of work on my upper body had marvelous results. After a certain point in our work together, you might want to consider trying the rolfing series yourself."

"That sounds good, but for now I think this is about all I can handle," says Jason. Then, after some reflection, he continues. "It's interesting what you said about the mechanical implications of chronic tension in the hip area. I was so involved with the emotional stuff coming up that I didn't much consider anything else."

Jason's Inner Child

"I was really amazed at how intensely I could feel that seven-year-old boy inside—how much he suffered and hated it when his dad whipped him," Jason explains. "And it was wonderful the way you suggested I go back in time as a wise and loving adult in his life, comfort him, and be the friend or parent he needed but didn't have back then. The way you coached me to build a time bridge between who I am now and the hurting child I was back then was really useful.

"One of the things I learned about myself in recovery is how I tend to be extreme in whatever I do. I think you must have intuited that when you warned me not to get lost in my inner child's pain. I needed to be reminded that I would be no good for him unless I could maintain a solid grounding in the compassion and wisdom I've learned in the last thirty years.

"For a while I was feeling terribly judgmental about myself for having ignored this hurting child inside all these years. I guess you sensed that because at one point in the massage, after I'd been crying, you pointed out that perhaps it had been necessary to learn how to be a good father to my two outer kids before I was able to tackle the job of reparenting my inner one."

A Time Bridge to Sealed Trauma

Sharon warmly receives Jason's wisdom. After a pause, she suggests, "Remember the idea of creating a time bridge between the present and the unhealed hurting times of the past? If you'd like, we could work with that a little more."

With Jason's nod of approval, Sharon continues. "One of the things that's impressed me so much as I participate in this inner child healing work is how the hurtful events themselves, horrible though they may be, are not the worst part of the trauma. The most damaging part seems to be how the pain gets sealed inside or turned back on the child. For instance, after father-daughter incest, it is common for the child to be told by her father that if she tells anyone, he'll kill her, or deny it and say she's lying, or even claim it was her flirtations that 'made him do it,' adding guilt and a false sense of responsibility to the trauma. So the wound is sealed, and it is often decades before circumstances arise that are safe enough to support an unsealing process and the recognition, acceptance, and integration that eventually lead to healing."

As she is talking, Jason is deep in thought. Sensing his need for time to process his own feelings, Sharon waits patiently. When his words are ready, Jason speaks. "What you were saying really hits home! I never minded the beatings I got nearly so much as my Dad's telling me how rotten I was, how it was my fault that he had to beat me, and how he had to do this for my own good. I think the damage to my self-esteem was much worse than to my body, even though I often had welts that lasted for days. I wanted to go to my mom and have her tell me everything would be OK, but I felt so vile that I didn't think I deserved even her love. So I just kept to myself, accepted as truth all those awful things my dad said about me, and hated myself."

Survival Instinct and Armoring

Sharon nods and adds, "Since all this was much more than you possibly could have handled consciously as a child, your survival instinct created armoring in the form of forgetfulness and chronic muscle tension so that you could somehow go on. It was the best you could do then Perhaps you'd like to send some thankfulness back in time to that wise boy who, by partially crippling himself emotionally and physically, survived and allowed you to be here today. And now, in addition to thankfulness, you have thirty years of additional experience and wisdom to contribute to the healing of this wounded inner child."

Just at the moment, Jason looks so much like the child he was describing that Sharon feels her own maternal instinct to nurture rising. While she feels strongly tempted to play out the role of the healing mother herself, her inner guidance suggests that it will be more beneficial for Jason to develop a stronger link with his own inner healing presence. Sharing this with him, they agree to explore further.

Introducing a Healing Presence

"Even though we can't undo the trauma of the past," says Sharon, "we can in a sense go back in time and introduce loving, healing elements to our 'stuck' places that will help loosen them and feed their further development inside. When you were young, did you have anyone who especially represented unconditional love for you?"

Jason's face lights up as he describes his piano teacher. Clara was a powerful and wise woman; her hour lessons were always the high point of his week.

"So now," continues Sharon, "perhaps you could remember and share with me one of those childhood beatings. But this time, instead of slinking off alone afterward, let's pretend that you run into Clara and, sensing that something's wrong, she invites you to her home for cookies, cocoa, and compassion."

For the next half hour, Sharon and Jason slowly and gently navigate the murky memories of pain and humiliation. As guide, Sharon sometimes plays the role of Clara, inserting warm, accepting, loving messages into the recesses where only self-condemnation and self-loathing have existed before.

From Talk to Touch

Eventually their dialogue reaches a resting point. Sharon then suggests they bring these newfound resources into the massage room and continue their "discussion" tactily. Before the bodywork begins, they both invite the healing presence of Clara to be present and ask that she continue to soothe and heal the memories stored in bodily tissue just as she has been doing with those stored in the mind.

As the massage unfolds, Jason finds it is much easier to access his once-hidden feelings of shame and fear. Time after time, as his body instinctively reacts by tightening, Sharon softly reminds him to talk to Clara inside, to seek her loving help, to listen to what she has to say. There are also several instances when, noticing Jason's resistance through hardening tissue, she encourages him to honor his need to protect what's inside, to only allow opening of what's ready to come into consciousness, and to set and maintain appropriate boundaries in their work together. She explains that she is not an "authority"—not an expert before whom Jason must surrender his sovereignty. Rather, she offers herself as a guide, as a facilitator of his own unique process. Always, she reminds him, he remains in charge.

Clara's Melting Love

As the session unfolds, Clara becomes an ever more vital presence in the room. Sometimes Sharon speaks out loud for her as a balance to Jason's enmeshment with his inner pain. Sometimes she reminds Jason to go to Clara, to allow her sweet love to soften and melt the hardness that is now no longer protective, but rather a burden and hinderance to the freedom and intimacy he longs for.

There are times when Jason is articulate and provides ongoing information to help Sharon follow his inner happenings. Other times he is silent, and Sharon is left to navigate using a sort of intuitive sonar she's developed over the years. She then follows her inner guidance as to how deep to go, how long to work in each area, and how to balance the energies of confrontation with compassion, of release with integration, of masculine with feminine.

When the bodywork is complete and Sharon is about to leave the room, she says, "Do take some time now and just be with the tender child inside, with Clara, and with the link you've opened between the present and where they live in the past. It's important to reassure them that you won't forget what you've learned today and that you'll keep this time bridge open. Remind them that you'll continue to visit them and actively participate in lovingly helping this inner lad grow toward the full, straight, beautiful manhood he was always destined to attain."

As she closes the door behind her, Sharon offers a silent prayer of thanks for being allowed to witness and participate in this transformational healing process. Sipping some juice while she waits for Jason, physically exhausted after this three-hour intensive, her heart sings in gladness for the new freedom and love that have been released into the world this day. In the spirit of midwives everywhere, she sighs in deep satisfaction and rejoices in the delight of new life.

The real voyage of discovery lies not in seeking new landscapes but in having new eyes.

—*Marcel Proust*

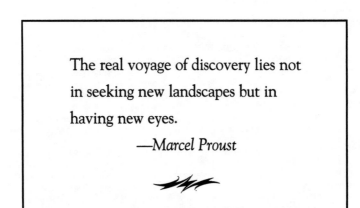

Egoholics Anonymous

Several weeks have passed since inner peace facilitator Sharon last worked with her client Jason (in the previous chapter). Today, as their session begins, they are discussing Jason's recovery from alcoholism.

After listening attentively for a while, Sharon says,"It's interesting, Jason, how much I can empathize with what you've been sharing about your recovery process, even though, as I mentioned, I've never been a drinker myself. But so many of my clients are in recovery from one addiction or another that I've come to learn a bit about the process."

Addiction to "Me"

"Over the years I've come to realize that I, too, have an addiction, even though there is no particular substance associated with it," Sharon explains. "As a spiritual seeker, my experiences have made it painfully clear how addicted I am to "Sharon," to identifying "me" with my personality. I have known for decades that my true essence—my spirit or soul—transcends this limited body/mind that I seem to be so fond of. Still, when I'm honest, I notice that my attachment to *who I think I am* is very similar to an alcoholic's attachment to drinking.

"Now, please don't misunderstand," she adds. "I'm not saying that ego itself is the problem—just excessive *identification* with it. We all need a certain amount of healthy ego in order to live on this planet. But in our culture, worshiping of individual egos has become elevated almost to the level of a religion. Questions like "What's in it for me?" and values like "Being number one is everything" or "Win at all costs" reflect this obsession with the importance of *my* individuality. We seem to collectively believe that it's crucial for individuals to succeed, even if our doing so individually causes suffering for others. This belief is reflected in the ways we do business, in how we organize sporting activities, and in numerous aspects of what we collectively and unconsciously take for granted as 'the way things are.'

"Now for what I'm saying to make sense, Jason, we have to remember that the essence of ego can operate on both individual and collective levels. For instance, what passes for nationalism these days is basically nationalistic ego, an identification with country in a way that accentuates our *separateness* from people of different countries. Likewise with racial, ethnic, or religious collective egos."

Distorting Perception

Jason is warming up to this line of thinking now. "So what you're saying," he adds, " is that the problem of ego isn't simply knowing who we are, either individually or as a group—it's *distorting* this knowing in a way that focuses on what *separates* us rather than acknowledging all that we have in common."

Sharon can't repress a huge grin as she says, "Boy, Jason, it sounds like you are in recovery from much more than just alcohol!"

"Of course," continues Jason, "this is what they mean in recovery circles when they say that you're either going forward or going backward. What I learned in my drinking years terrified me so deeply that I won't risk ever going backward again. So I keep going forward, questioning, trying to understand the way things really are at deeper and deeper levels. It's actually kind of fun!"

Ego's Myopia

"I've also thought a lot about ego and the line between a healthy expression of who I am and an unhealthy obsession with 'me,'" Jason says. "Near as I can understand it, excessive involvement with 'me' is a kind of myopia, a nearsightedness that leaves everyone and everything else in the world out of focus. In this state, I can't see well enough to avoid bumping into others and hurting myself. It's really a very contracted kind of consciousness, one that has to see life through a lens of fear and distrust. So I end up walking through my days artificially ignorant, defended, and . . . recreating all the chronic tension we've been working so hard to release these past few sessions.

"Then sometimes I get thinking about the values we *say* are so important: cooperation, caring for others, unselfishness. These sound great, but they're really in direct conflict with the interests of my myopic ego."

Sharon is so delighted at the direction this dialogue is taking that she surrenders to a whimsical voice inside that says, "Jason, the similarity between substance abuse and ego abuse is so strong that at times I've considered forming a group and calling it something like 'Egoholics Anonymous.' We could have meetings and share how our true, meaningful development has become arrested because of our addiction to the illusion of an all-important 'me.'"

An Egoholic Twelve-Step Program

"Oh yeah," retorts Jason with a grin, "I could be a charter member of *that* group! With a few minor variations, I can just see us working the twelve steps:

1. We admitted we were powerless over our ego cravings—that maintaining our spirit's inherent clarity and balance in our lives had become unmanageable.

2. We came to believe that a power greater than ourselves could restore us to sanity."

"I hear about such spiritual awakenings from so many clients these days," says Sharon. "While there may be a bit of shyness until we really get into the topic, I find that most of the people I work with are quite willing to bring a higher power into this work. Some need a little help clarifying what form or name feels best for them, that's all. But when they're clear that I'm not trying to sell them any particular religion, their own sense of 'something greater' usually reveals itself.

"This is fun, Jason! Would it be useful for your work today to continue with the rest of the steps?"

"Yes, definitely! I told you that as a recovering addict, I need to keep on going forward. Since I've already proven to myself how useful the twelve-step approach is in one kind of recovery, let's see if it can be equally useful in recovering spiritual sobriety."

"Working" Spiritual Sobriety

Jason was eager to go on:

"3. We made a decision to turn our will and lives over to the care of God *as we understood him/her/it.*

I guess that's what you were just describing—how you help clients clarify their understanding of God. Yes, that's right on track!

4. We made a searching and fearless moral inventory of ourselves.

Hmmm . . . That's sort of what we're starting to do in these sessions together, isn't it?"

"You bet," replies Sharon. "As I understand it, the word *moral* refers to being *able to distinguish* between right and wrong. This gets us back to the question of values and how we handle conflict when we discover we hold opposing values inside."

"Well, maybe," adds Jason, "that's why we need an Egoholics Anonymous group as a place to explore with other egoholics the nature of right and wrong as we begin to evolve out of our egocentric morality. I think the sense of what's right for a person who's looking out for number one must be very different from what's right for a person committed to a life of cooperation with others, expanding consciousness, and inner peace.

"One of the reasons why I've continued coming here is that this kind of bodywork is very much like a fearless moral inventory. Your hands function as a kind of mirror, reflecting into my awareness hidden blockages, feelings, and memories that I need to integrate if I'm ever to be fully successful in my recovery."

"Sounds like we're right on track," says Sharon. "What's next?"

Wrongs and Woundedness

"The next one is really hard for me," sighs Jason:

"5. We admitted to God, to ourselves, and to another human being the exact nature of our wrongs.

That's definitely important, but somehow I like your gentler approach of first experiencing the *nature of my woundedness* and trying to help my inner child heal from the traumas of the past. I think that as that happens, the hardened pain that was compelling my wrong behaviors will naturally soften, release, and cease to be such a problem."

Delighting in the wisdom of her student, Sharon beams and encourages him to continue. Jason then offers:

> "6. We were entirely ready to have God remove all these defects of character.

Oh, yes, and I also have to remember that 'God helps those who help themselves'—and those who sincerely and appropriately seek help from others.

> 7. We humbly asked God to remove our shortcomings.
>
> 8. We made a list of all persons we had harmed and became willing to make amends to them all."

Making Amends

Jason pauses and looks a bit downcast. After a few moments he says, "That's a hard one. When I worked this step as an alcoholic, I really could list most of those I'd hurt because of my drinking. But I can't even imagine everyone I've harmed because of my self-centeredness and egoistic myopia."

Sharon also feels the weight of this step. After a time of mutual reflection, she tentatively suggests, "Maybe for our Egoholics Anonymous work we can soften this one a bit so that the focus is on inner transformation that changes our behavior *from this moment on.* For myself, I think the law of cause and effect will take care of bringing back to me the results of my past self-centered behavior. I just want to be able to accept my karma in whatever way it unfolds with awareness and thankfulness—and a continuing eagerness to learn from whatever happens!"

"That makes sense to me," says Jason, smiling. "What you're saying is expressed slightly differently in the next two steps:

9. We made direct amends to such people wherever possible except when to do so would injure them or others.

10. We continued to take personal inventory and when we were wrong promptly admitted it."

"This is wonderful, Jason. I had no idea these twelve-step programs were based on such deep wisdom."

"People's ignorance of the power of this work outside of recovery circles is tragic," sighs Jason. "But maybe that's because most of us are so busy denying those parts of our lives that might benefit from recovery!"

Recovery and Prayer

"I think you'll really like the last two steps," Jason enthuses. "They sound just like what you've been saying all along:

11. We sought through prayer and meditation to improve our conscious contact with God *as we understood him/her/it*, praying only for knowledge of God's will for us and the power to carry it out.

12. Having had a spiritual awakening as the result of these steps, we tried to carry this message to egoholics and to practice these principles in all our affairs."

"That's magnificent, Jason," exclaims Sharon. "Thank you so much for sharing this with me! It helps to understand what I'm offering here as part of a much larger recovery movement. I've always known that the muscular tension that brings most of my clients in for work is only a symptom of much deeper dis-ease. And I've seen how this dis-ease arises out of unhealed inner wounds and conflicting values that aren't even recognized and hence can't be dealt with effectively. What you've just shown me, though, is that the transpersonal, spiritual focus of this work has repeatedly proven its power to heal in millions of people who have freed themselves from addictions with the help of the recovery community and reliance on something greater than any ego can ever provide."

"That's right," agrees Jason. "And one of the ways this blessing keeps growing is reflected in a favorite AA saying: 'Pass it on.'"

Needless to say, the bodywork that follows has a wonderfully transcendent quality to it. Jason remains in an almost continuous state of prayerful receptivity to the transforming power of divine will. Sharon likewise remains focused on her intention that her hands and words be a clear conduit for transformative healing.

Perhaps this, they each wonder, is one way an Egoholics Anonymous meeting might unfold. And also, they realize, this is definitely a way God can bring forth the divine qualities latent within each human—one body at a time.

For additional information on AA, you can contact Alcoholics Anonymous World Service, Inc., at P.O. Box 459, Grand Central Station, New York, NY 10163; (212) 870-3400.

The conclusion is always the same: love is the most powerful and still the most unknown energy in the world.

—*Pierre Teilhard de Chardin*

TWENTY

What We Offer Is Who We Are

A Practitioner-Supervisor Dialogue

One of the recurring themes in this book is that the source of our healing abilities is *who we are,* not just what we know. A complementary theme has been the importance for inner peace facilitators to continue and deepen their own inner work. This might include regular meditation practice, hatha yoga, journal writing, awareness-oriented martial arts training, personal-growth workshops, spiritual practices, and professional supervision.

The importance of regular supervision for inner peace facilitators is discussed in appendix A, emphasizing the benefit to a practitioner of an ongoing relationship with a trusted wise-person familiar with your work. This person acts as a regular and reliable "mirror" to help you see and work with personal issues that can create difficulties in client relationships *before* they become problematic. This person could be a psychotherapist, a senior practitioner of your modality, a spiritual guide, or a religious counselor.

The term *supervisor* is used to refer to someone with whom you can discuss the specifics of your client relationships *without violating confidentiality.* However, given the nature of our current legal climate and the potential for liability associated with "professional supervision," a cautious provider might prefer that such a relationship be called a mentorship or simply "personal counseling."

Sharon's Supervision Relationship

To bring alive the nature of the practitioner-supervisor relationship—an issue that often engenders resistance and denial in practitioners—let us listen in on part of a session with Sharon, the fictional practitioner of the previous two chapters, and her supervisor, Patricia. They have been meeting weekly for almost three years now. While Sharon began seeing Patricia because of a potentially messy situation with an emotionally unbalanced client, her growing appreciation of Patricia's experience, skill, and mentoring capacities have kept Sharon coming back. Difficulties in finding the time and money for this ongoing work have often tempted her to quit or come less often. When this happens, though, consulting her inner guidance reveals that these "realities" usually occur along with her resistance to dealing with some painful unconscious pattern that is just about to surface.

In her clear moments, Sharon is tremendously grateful for these weekly sessions. Patricia is a highly trained and intuitive psychotherapist with a background in body-oriented modalities. In their work together, Patricia combines the roles of therapist and supervisor as she assists Sharon in understanding both her own inner processes (such as projecting blocked feelings onto others) and those of her clients. With skillful questioning, clear psychodynamic models, and a wealth of relevant personal experience to share, Patricia has a masterful ability to "be present with" whatever's happening in a spacious and supportive manner, usually with an invitingly curious twinkle dancing in her eye.

Experiencing Past Fears

Since their work together integrates both psychotherapeutic counseling for Sharon as a person and professional supervision for Sharon as a practitioner, part of each session involves "checking in" and discovering which issues most need attention. Today Sharon has been airing her fear of getting in over her head as she helps her clients unravel their various issues.

"Even though I make it very clear from the beginning that I am *not* a psychotherapist," says Sharon, "and I explain the difference between that kind of work and inner peace counseling, still I often find myself coming perilously close to the edge of my competence."

Patricia nods and asks, "Can you recall how you feel when you notice this happening, Sharon?"

"Oh, yes," she replies, "I get a tightness in my stomach. I feel like a little kid playing someplace dangerous, and I'm afraid my daddy is going to find me and yell at me. I hated it when he did that!"

For a while, Patricia acts as a "healer's healer." Helping Sharon explore her past, together they create a healing crucible for old wounds to be seen, accepted, and lovingly integrated into present reality. This, Sharon knows, is also a vital part of a well-orchestrated supervision session and becomes a container for the work she is then able to do with her clients.

Beth's Sexuality

As Sharon becomes able to separate more clearly her current realities from the shadows of past fears, Patricia returns the dialogue to the concern that began the session. "Is there a client with whom you are particularly concerned about crossing the boundary from counseling to psychotherapy, Sharon?"

Sharon nods and tries to explain. "I've been working with Beth for six sessions now. I feel we've established a pretty good rapport and have felt confident in our work together. Then yesterday, during the bodywork, Beth was opening to the feelings of the eight-year-old girl inside her. It was so clear: as she cried—remembering being abused by her father—the sobs were very different from what I had heard from her before. If I played you a recording of them, you'd swear you were listening to a child."

"It sounds like she was dissociating and regressing," comments Patricia. "Was this the first time this has happened in your work together?"

"I think so," says Sharon. "But then Beth's body began to move in ways that made me uncomfortable. I had been releasing some deeply held memories in her gluteal muscles when the crying began. Realizing that the energy was that of a child in pain, I held her hand, moved more slowly, and generally surrounded her with loving acceptance and support. Her movements, though, had a distinctly sexual feeling to them. I even wondered if she were stimulating herself on the table. Part of me wanted to pull away from her and felt judgmental about what she was doing. But another part could see that this was really age-appropriate behavior for this child who had been confused by sexual messages from her father and had no adult who could help her sort out her feelings. Part of me wanted to embrace her and tell her that everything would be OK. But another part wanted to tell her to get a grip on herself and stop moving in such a sexual way—she was making me uncomfortable.

"I think what ended up happening worked out fine. I didn't give in to either impulse, but just stayed connected with her. Sometimes I was holding her hand patiently, sometimes the massage continued—but much less deeply. Gradually the sexual motions subsided. Both of us, though, seemed embarrassed to talk about want had happened. I really don't want this to become a distancing factor in our relationship, but I'm not sure if I can bring up the topic and maintain my own equilibrium."

Sharon's Supervisor Responds

Patricia's face is radiant. For a fleeting moment, she reminds Sharon of a mother whose darling child has just won a coveted prize. Having feared reproach from her mentor, she wonders why Patricia seems so happy.

"I think you handled a very difficult situation quite well," says Patricia. "And the way you have presented your concerns just now reveals a level of professional maturity and development that brings joy to my heart."

After a few moments of shared warmth, Patricia asks, "Did you get the feeling that the adult Beth was at all present while the sexual motions were happening? If so, then your nonjudgmental presence could have acted as a container for her confusion, arousal, and embarrassment. Or did you sense that she was totally disidentified from the repressed child feelings that were being released in her body?"

"I'm not clear about that," responds Sharon. "But first of all, I think I'd better look at my own reactions to watching Beth's sexual movements. My inner therapist suggests that I'm probably carrying some negative judgments about expressing *my own* sexuality. I really want to be able to keep *my* issues separate from my work with Beth in the future."

"Excellent!" says Patricia. "This is one of the most difficult challenges we face when we work with others at such an intimate level. Even after all my years of training and experience, I'm still far from perfect at this. But I have gotten much more skillful at noticing when my patterns are influencing my perceptions and evaluations with a client. Therefore, I can deal with them more consciously and do what it takes to get the necessary clarity as I determine appropriate boundaries for working together."

The remainder of this session continues an exploration of Sharon's issues concerning sexual expression that have surfaced from time to time in past years. Arising as they have in the context of professional supervision, though, Sharon feels especially motivated to become clear so that her "stuff" doesn't interfere with her intuition or distort her judgment when she's facilitating Beth's healing.

With Patricia now in the role of psychotherapist, Sharon focuses fully on being "the client." Together they investigate the hidden wells of feeling, old festering wounds, and ongoing ambivalence that have so long confused and limited her. Knowing that this work is both for her own healing *and* for Beth's, Sharon seeks deeper access to her inner reservoir of courage and wisdom. And as their session comes to a close, she trusts that Patricia's guidance and her own evolving thirst for clarity will support her for as long as this process takes.

Determining Appropriate Boundaries

In the following week's session, Sharon once more brings up her work with Beth, still feeling unclear about boundaries in that relationship. She relates how when they met a few days back, both of them unconsciously colluded to keep sexual issues from entering their work.

"I think," begins Patricia, "that there are three questions that are useful in determining appropriate boundaries in counseling work generally. Let's play with them and see if they help in this instance.

"First of all, in this particular part of your client's healing process, do you feel you have something of value to offer? In this situation, this might mean taking into account all you know about Beth, yourself, and especially the sexual issues we discussed last week.

"If the answer to that is yes, then the second general question concerns how confident you are in your abilities to catch and deal with your client's projections onto you and also your projections and reactions with her. These are called 'transference' and 'countertransference' in psychotherapy and are extremely challenging arenas for maintaining consciousness. All counselors end up having to deal with these issues in their client relationships to some degree, but beyond a certain point this is work for a trained psychotherapist. Where that point is in any given situation, though, is your judgment call."

"I think," says Sharon, "that with some more work like we did last week, I'll be able to maintain my clarity and hold open a safe space for Beth to continue her explorations. I know she trusts me, and I think she is ready and able to deepen her relationship with that wounded little girl inside."

"Very good," says Patricia. "Then you've pretty much answered the third question also. This concerns your client's ability and readiness to integrate the split-off child self and her more mature adult self. Again, this is a judgment call. More complex situations require the skills of an experienced psychotherapist; with a relatively functional and mature individual, the fruits of your compassion and experience may be just what's called for. In dealing with Beth, for instance, you said last week that when her sexual movements were occurring, you felt she was like a child of about eight years old."

Sharon nods and says, "Part of me was delighted that she trusted me enough to allow such uninhibited expression of this split-off part of herself. It really felt quite innocent—a natural and healthy childlike expression of feelings. I was reminded of what I've seen my daughter doing at times. I just wish I had been able to simply hold open a safe space for Beth to physically and emotionally experience her inner child's energy. Maybe then I could also have helped her create a bridge from her adult self to this child inside who is so in need of acceptance and understanding. Then Beth would have been better able to understand and integrate these different parts of herself and hopefully bring more awareness to her choices for expression. But I'm afraid my own 'stuff' got in the way."

Sharon Works with Her Own Inner Child Conflicts

"That may have been the case last time," says Patricia with a tender look, "but with what I've seen of your commitment to your own maturing process, this won't be the situation for long! Now, what about the little girl inside of *you*? From the way you've been talking, you're apparently not so generous in accepting *her* expression of sexual feelings."

"But I'm an adult," protests Sharon. "I should know better!"

"Does being adult mean suppressing your inner child?" asks Patricia gently. "Or might a better definition be 'one who lovingly and skillfully accepts and *integrates* each aspect of herself according to the values and wisdom she has developed over a lifetime'?"

Patricia is now quiet, simply being present for Sharon as she struggles with her inner conflicts. Finally there's a release as Sharon laughs and says, "It's so funny: I can really see myself embracing and loving my inner child in her curious explorations. And at the same time, there's an adult inside who's blaming and hurting her for not suppressing her free-flowing sexuality. No wonder adults drive children crazy!"

"Not adults such as you are at this moment," replies Patricia. "The real crazy-making energy comes from an adult's *denial* of inner conflicts, not just from the mere existence of conflict. Children fortunate enough to grow up around adults such as yourself who are exploring, owning, and healing their inner worlds are much more likely to absorb a sense of integrity, a willingness to deal with uncomfortable feelings, and a playful interest in all facets of their lives."

"That's the kind of adult behavior I would like to be modeling for all of my clients," says Sharon. "Especially Beth. Let's see if we can use the rest of this session to deal with whatever is hampering my ability to fully support Beth in this part of her work."

Seeking Balance

For the remainder of this session and several that follow, Sharon grapples with each of the questions Patricia has put forth. It's a delicate balance she's seeking. Clearly, if she misappraises her abilities and gets in over her head, she could end up deepening and further binding her client's trauma rather than freeing it. But if she is excessively cautious, refusing to support Beth as she vulnerably reaches out for help, a precious opportunity for healing could be lost.

Over years of absorbing wisdom from her mentor, Sharon has come to learn that there are rarely absolute answers to her most difficult problems with clients. Rather, Patricia has taught her the art of feeling her way into her inner reality, of simultaneously experiencing conflicting feelings and beliefs, and of containing the accompanying anxiety so that decisions are not forced before this wisdom-distillation process can produce them naturally.

There are certainly many moments when Sharon doubts her sanity and wonders if inner peace facilitation isn't just a fancy label for meddling in other people's lives. Yet when she examines these doubts in the light of her expanding abilities as a truth seeker, her inner counselor assures her that her motives *are* growing purer month by month, that what she offers *does* indeed have enduring value to her clients, and that her deepening sense of humility *is* a wonderful protection against the worst excesses of the healing arts.

And, finally, Sharon is coming to realize that there can never be complete safety in her work—that it will always be a balancing act between conflicting realities. Just as a tightrope walker must know how to deal with the inevitable falls skillfully and with a minimum of harm, so does Sharon realize that she must remain ever vigilant and prepared to find herself lost in uncharted territories. Accepting that she may never feel secure as an inner peace facilitator, Sharon nonetheless continues, embracing her training and the ongoing gifts of her wonderful mentor in a spirit of joyful adventure and deep appreciation.

The thoughts and discussions presented in this chapter have been offered to inspire, invite contemplation, and help differentiate between the work of an inner peace facilitator and a psychotherapist/professional supervisor. Their purpose is to demonstrate how psychotherapeutic supervision can benefit a facilitator; they are not meant to suggest that one should practice psychotherapy without appropriate training. Inner peace facilitators are cautioned not to confuse the exchanges between Patricia and Sharon (which are psychotherapy) with other kinds of client-practitioner discussions suggested for inner peace facilitation.

Let's not look back in anger,

or forward in fear,

but around in awareness.

—*James Thurber*

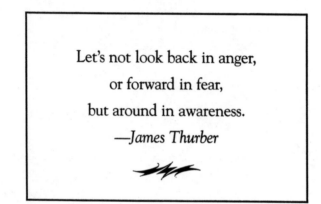

Onward

Resources along the Path

Transformation Through Bodywork really has no conclusion. The processes described are ongoing, opening both recipients and practitioners to new dimensions of awareness, skill, and joy as they pursue the mysteries inherent in the quest for inner peace.

Through all the various explorations in this book, I hope one point has remained clear: there *is* something greater than what our day-to-day consciousness reveals. Regardless of what we call it, this source of wisdom becomes available to each of us as we "do the work" and become more attuned to its guidance. This work, of course, is a lifelong affair. My hope is that the insights in this book have given you some small assistance for part of your journey.

As you continue unfolding your own unique growth process, the following resources mentioned in the text (plus a few additional suggestions) may be useful. These have all been sources of inspiration for me and have helped shape the ideas developed in this book. It is a brief list; please note that several books offer more comprehensive reference sections and are marked with an asterisk (*).

Though I suspect few of us will have easy journeys in the years to come, hanging out with some of these writers and explorers can ease life's trials and tribulations by providing a larger context for understanding and accepting what is happening. Many different points of view are represented, but all have in common processes that expand consciousness and have much nourishment for the wisdom growing inside of you.

173

May your inner guide reveal what will be most useful to you at the time when you are most ready to receive it.

Books and Tapes:
Psychology, Consciousness, and Spirituality

The Common Boundary Graduate Education Guide: Holistic Programs and Resources Integrating Spirituality and Psychology*
Common Boundary, Dept. GEG, 5272 River Rd., Suite 650, Bethesda, MD 20816. An invaluable resource for those seeking formal psychological training.

Dawning: Eternal Wisdom—Heritage for Today
By Swami Amar Jyoti. Truth Consciousness, Inc., at Sacred Mountain Ashram, 10668 Gold Hill Rd., Boulder, CO 80302; (303) 447-1637. An inspiring collection of wisdom teachings deeply applicable to inner peace facilitation.

Fire in the Soul: A New Psychology of Spiritual Optimism*
Guilt Is the Teacher, Love Is the Lesson*
Minding the Body, Mending the Mind*
The Power of the Mind to Heal: Renewing Body, Mind, and Spirit*
By Joan Borysenko. Body/Mind Health Sciences, Inc., 393 Dixon Rd., Boulder, CO 80302-7177; (303) 440-8460, fax (303) 440-7580. These outstanding books are inspiring and nurturing aides to healing arts professionals and spiritual seekers; the first one has been especially meaningful to this practitioner. Excellent resource sections.

Forgiveness: A Bold Choice for a Peaceful Heart*
By Robin Casarjian. Bantam Books, 666 5th Ave., New York, NY 10103.

The Global Brain: Speculations on the Evolutionary Leap to Planetary Consciousness*
A White Hole in Time*
By Peter Russell. Jeremy P. Tarcher, Inc., 9110 Sunset Blvd., Los Angleles, CA 90069. Excellent lucid explorations from an evolu-

tionary perspective of the nature and destiny of the human race. Great for providing a context for what many readers are experiencing currently.

Grace Unfolding: Psychotherapy in the Spirit of the Tao-te ching
By Greg Johanson and Ron Kurtz. Bell Tower, 201 East 50th St., New York, NY 10022. An excellent exploration of Taoist philosophy as applicable to healing arts professionals. (See chapter 15 for excerpt.)

Gradual Awakening
Healing into Life and Death
Guided Meditation, Explorations and Healings
By Stephen Levine. Warm Rock Tapes, P.O. Box 108, Chamisal, NM 87521. A consistently rewarding and easy-to-digest source of spiritual and psychological guidance.

Healing Words: The Power of Prayer and the Practice of Medicine
By Larry Dossey. Harper San Francisco, 1160 Battery St., San Francisco, CA 94111; (415) 447-4400. An engrossing review of the medical research on the scientific effects of prayer on healing.

How Can I Help?: Stories and Reflections on Service
By Ram Dass and Paul Gorman. Alfred A. Knopf, Inc., 201 E. 50th St., New York, NY 10022. An exploration of why we participate in "doing good" and how we can purify ourselves so that our good intentions have their intended results.

Leadership and the New Science: Learning about Organization from an Orderly Universe
By Margaret J. Wheatley. Berrett-Koehler Publishers, Inc., 155 Montgomery St., San Francisco, CA 94104; (415) 288-0260, fax (415) 362-2512.

A Little Book on the Human Shadow
By Robert Bly. HarperCollins Publishers, 10 E. 53rd St., New York, NY 10022. Chapters 2 and 3 offer an especially vivid description of

the process of reclaiming our shadow energy and consciousness so that we can use them in support of our life's work.

The Paths of Yoga

By Sri Kriyananda. Crystal Clarity Publications, 14618 Tyler Foote Rd., Nevada City, CA 95959; (800) 424-1055. Excerpts from Lessons in Yoga: 14 Steps to Higher Awareness. Publisher also offers a variety of books, tapes, and lessons supporting spiritual growth.

Peace Pilgrim: Her Life and Work in Her Own Words

Friends of Peace Pilgrim, 43480 Cedar Ave., Hemet, CA 92544; (909) 927-7678. This all-volunteer operation distributes a variety of publications and tapes about Peace Pilgrim.

Psychotherapy: The Art of Wooing Nature

By Sheldon Roth. Jason Aronson, Inc., 230 Livingston St., Northvale, NJ 07647. An academic but readable intellectual approach to psychological issues many practitioners encounter with clients.

Ram Dass Tapes and Books

Hanuman Foundation Tape Library, 524 San Anselmo Ave., Suite 203, San Anselmo, CA 94960; (800) 248-1008, fax (415) 454-4143. Publishes a catalog describing Ram Dass's talks and related offerings; wonderfully inspiring wisdom teachings.

Riding the Tiger: Doing Business in a Transforming World

By Harrison Owen. Abbott Publishing, 7808 River Falls Dr., Potomac, MD 20854; (301) 469-9269. A powerful bridge for communication with clients working within organizations, especially dysfunctional ones; mind-expanding visions for deepening understanding.

Strategy of the Dolphin: Scoring a Win in a Chaotic World

By Dudly Lynch and Paul L. Kordis. Ballantine Books, 201 E. 50th St., New York, NY 10022. A rather technical but invigorating ride through consciousness, innovation, chaos, management theory, and the purpose of life. Excellent material for helping business-oriented clients expand consciousness and develop intellectual understanding of inner peace as understood by advanced business thinkers.

Books and Tapes:
Simple Living and Financial Issues

Gesundheit!: Bringing Good Health to You, the Medical System, and Society through Physician Service, Complementary Therapies, Humor, and Joy

By Patch Adams. Healing Arts Press, One Park St., Rochester, VT 05767. Patch Adams is one of the most outspoken advocates of healers separating access to their services from their client's ability to pay. A moving and inspiring account of his life and the cooperative work of many to create a free hospital in West Virginia.

How Much Is Enough?: The Consumer Society and the Future of the Earth

By Alan Durning. The Worldwatch Institute, 1776 Massachusetts Ave. NW, Washington, D.C. 20036. Strong support for thinking through the differences between needs and desires and in bringing lifestyle choices in harmony with deeply held inner beliefs.

Network to Reduce Overconsumption: A Directory of Organizations and Leaders

The New Road Map Foundation, P.O. Box 15981, Seattle, WA 98115; (206) 527- 0437. Detailed information on more than a hundred organizations providing information, training, and support for lifestyle simplification; many offer useful newsletters.

Voluntary Simplicity: Toward a Way of Life That Is Outwardly Simple, Inwardly Rich

By Duane Elgin. William Morrow and Company, Inc., 1350 Ave. of the Americas, New York, NY 10019. A wonderful, readable, compassionate discussion of issues affecting our lifestyle choices and their resulting needs for certain levels of income.

Your Money or Your Life: Transforming Your Relationship with Money and Achieving Financial Independence
By Joe Dominguez and Vickie Robin. Viking Penguin, 375 Hudson St., New York, NY 10014. A useful and encouraging exploration of money and its meaning in our lives. (See appendix B: "Considering the Relative Worth of the Client's and Practitioner's Time.")

Periodicals

Common Boundary: Exploring Spirituality, Psychotherapy, and Creativity
P.O. Box 445, Mt. Morris, IL 61054-7819; (800) 548-8737. An excellent ongoing exploration of these rich and fascinating topics.

The Family Therapy Networker
8528 Bradford Rd., Silver Springs, MD 20901-9955; (301) 589-6536.

In Context: A Quarterly of Humane Sustainable Culture
P.O. Box 11470, Bainbridge Island, WA 98110; (800) IN CONTEXT. An excellent, reliable source of well-written, intelligent, multiperspective collections of articles on issues affecting our individual and collective peace; contains no advertising.

Intuition: A Magazine for the Higher Potential of the Mind
P.O. Box 460773, San Francisco, CA 94146; (415) 949-4240, fax (415) 917-8905. Fascinating articles exploring the practical use of intuition and honoring it as an important part of our information-gathering and decision-making abilities.

Light of Consciousness: A Journal of Spiritual Awakening
Desert Ashram, 3403 W. Sweetwater Dr., Tucson, AZ 85745; (602) 743-0384. An excellent source of inspiration and gentle guidance for unfolding spiritual consciousness; nondenominational, universal approach to the inner awakening process.

Massage magazine

1315 West Mallon, Spokane, WA 99201; subscriptions (800) 533-4263. A magazine that regularly features excellent articles and columns on the spiritual and transformational aspects of hands-on professional work.

Massage Therapy Journal

AMTA, 820 Davis St., Suite 100, MTJ Subscription, Evanston, IL 60201-4444; (708) 864-0123, fax (708) 864-1178. Especially note the article "Dual Relationships and Other Ethical Considerations" in the spring 1992 issue.

Organizations

The Guild of (financially) Accessible Practitioners

See appendix B. For current information, call (888) 2-THE GAP.

The Transformation Oriented Bodywork Network (TOB-Net)

Mickey McGinnis, Coordinator, P.O. Box 24967, San Jose, CA 95154-4967; (408) 371-6716. Distributes a quarterly newsletter, a directory of member profiles, and information on training opportunities in this new and rapidly evolving orientation to professional bodywork.

I have discovered that if I lead a life
of service to my fellow human
beings, honestly devoting my all to
that purpose, I never have to worry
about being taken care of myself.
Countless experiences have taught
me the value of compassion.
—*Wally Amos*

APPENDIXES

The material in these appendixes was written specifically for bodywork practitioners as support for dealing with a variety of issues associated with the professional practice of inner peace facilitation.

Those of us who have been on a spiritual path of consciousness know how it works. We know that when we make some changes internally they are immediately reflected in our life. Everything shifts. We need to understand how powerful that is. We really do affect the world—each one of us—when we do that transformational process in ourselves. That's really the most powerful effect we can have on the world. Then we can do things like taking political and social action. Those things are important. But if we take external action on the basis of being committed to our own growth process, it's much more powerful than if we're just projecting the problem outside of ourselves. We need to understand that our society is a reflection of consciousness. As our consciousness changes, our experience of life shifts.

—*Shakti Gawain*

Comparing Inner Peace Facilitation and Psychotherapy

A Practitioner's Guide to Similarities and Differences

Introduction

"I've been having so much trouble relating to my husband lately," lamented Susan as we spoke briefly at the beginning of her bodywork session. "When he's about to arrive home I can feel my tension level rising. I love him, but sometimes I think I'm going to go crazy if . . ."

A gentle silence fills the room as she stares at the floor. Part of me is eager to jump in with questions, to "help" in some direct way. Part of me is afraid to let this silence continue, afraid to feel my own resonating sadness and fear. And part of me is practicing my own inner peace techniques—calmly waiting, lovingly offering Susan all the time she might need to continue her inner work in an atmosphere free of judgment and full with acceptance.

As she finds words to express and clarify her inner confusion, I gently hold her in my heart, listen, and occasionally offer an insight as suggested by my inner guidance. Then at the appropriate time we move to the waiting bodywork table. As my hands mirror and release previously inaccessible feelings into Susan's consciousness, I feel her focus and relaxation deepen. By the end of the session, she seems to be a different person: more poised, peaceful, thinking and speaking more clearly, and expressing eagerness to bring her new awareness and understanding to this evening's dinner with her husband.

So what do we call this kind of work? Is it counseling bodywork? Body-centered or body-oriented psychotherapy? Inner peace facilitation integrated with transformation-oriented bodywork? Defining edges are not always clear, and work that includes both structured touch and verbal counseling is evolving rapidly, with many overlapping modalities, techniques, orientations, labels, and trademarks.

Definitions

One definition of psychotherapy is that it is a *systematic* approach to change and growth, as opposed to inner peace facilitation, which is a less structured sharing of accumulated wisdom and intuitive guidance. Another kind of distinction comes from Stephen Levine, author of *A Gradual Awakening* and *Healing Into Life and Death*. He contrasts psychotherapy with spiritual counseling, and after describing the process of noticing thoughts arising in the mind, he observes that psychotherapy focuses on the *content* of these thoughts, analyzing it, understanding its dynamics, and attempting to control or change it. By contrast, he says, spirituality is much more interested in the *space* in which these thoughts arise and asserts that "who I am" is much more (and inherently a different sort of stuff) than thoughts or mind.

As used in this book, inner peace facilitation is an *orientation* that is inherently spiritual in that it seeks to assist each client in becoming increasingly aware of inner spaciousness. Since spirit can be thought of as unbound space, spiritual counseling parallels and wonderfully complements the bodywork, which focuses on physical relaxation, freeing up energy, and reducing restrictions.

Soften and Melt

As "lay" counselors (in the sense of not possessing a qualifying academic degree and/or psychological licensing), we work with "functional" clients—people who possess a reasonable degree of mental health and are capable of accepting responsibility for their life's decisions. Our focus is not on the pathological, but on supporting functional individuals as they seek deeper awareness of their mental and emotional processes and their physical tension patterns. We work with softening and melting habits of the mind, heart, and body that block the shining forth of our client's natural inner peace.

The crucial words here are *soften* and *melt*. (Reminiscent of massage school?) It is strongly advised that we avoid implying psychological expertise and leave overly "hard" cases that are not appropriate for our softening and melting skills to therapists with different training.

While these definitions are somewhat arbitrary, they are meant as guidelines to help establish more clarity as we develop a scope of practice that is appropriate for our own unique background, abilities, and limitations. As we integrate into our work some of the principles and forms of interaction that have traditionally "belonged" to psychotherapy, it is most important to also maintain a sense of humility, a sense of appropriate limitation in our work. In support of this process, I strongly recommend ongoing education in psychology, spiritual disciplines, and other areas that complement and help us more clearly define our own offerings.

One periodical that I have found to be especially useful for this purpose is the *Family Therapy Networker* (see resources in chapter 21). While centered around the discipline of family therapy, it regularly presents articles illuminating issues affecting *any* counselor. It offers a strong feminist awareness and refreshingly humble discussions of just what therapy can and cannot accomplish. Main themes of previous issues include "Sexuality and the Family," "When Lightning Strikes: Trauma and Its Aftermath," "The Ethical Therapist: It's Hard to Be a White Knight in a Gray World," "Psychotherapy and Spirituality," "When Therapy Does Harm," "Incest," and "Money."

Shared Areas of Concern

Some areas of concern shared by both psychotherapists and inner peace facilitators include:

❖ Scope of practice
❖ Confidentiality
❖ Source of authority
❖ The practitioner as role model
❖ The practitioner as educator
❖ Awareness of transference and countertransference
❖ Containment and appropriate boundaries
❖ Client-centered session time

❖ Dual relationships
❖ Professional supervision

As we explore each of these areas, you might notice your own policies, practices, orientations, and beliefs and ask if they are serving your highest purpose as an inner peace facilitator.

Scope of Practice

The most important and absolutely vital need of all who offer healing assistance is *knowing your scope of practice*. This means honestly answering these questions: What level of competence do I have to offer in each of the various aspects of my work? Where are the "edges" beyond which there is too much danger for both myself as practitioner and for my vulnerable and trusting client? This can also be called working with my professional boundary issues, discovering my own abilities (or lack thereof), and learning restraint when interactions with clients take me too close to my competence boundary.

For instance, in the anecdote at the beginning of this chapter, Susan responded wonderfully to the facilitator's suggestions and left the session feeling more peaceful. It might have turned out differently, though. If you had been facilitating that session, would you have known what to do if Susan had become increasingly agitated during your discussion? What choices might you have made if the bodywork continued or perhaps increased her ill feelings about herself and her relationship? Would your experience to date have prepared you for guiding her through this kind of awkward session? Would you have been able to suggest further assistance for Susan if she was about to leave frustrated and unclear about how to proceed?

Counseling professionals who have undergone thorough, systematic training have, hopefully, learned to recognize and honor their own personal limitations. They have been taught contraindications for their specific forms of healing work, and they have been exposed to the offerings of other disciplines so that they might refer out as appropriate. Since we as lay counselors may not have experienced such systematic training, wisdom and common sense suggest that we proceed with caution, make conservative estimates of our abilities, and limit our work with each client to approaches we know from our own experience to be effective and for which we feel able to handle the problems that may arise.

Wise though it is not to overestimate our skills, it is also important not to be overly meek or grovel before an assumed superiority of psychotherapy. As a healing arts professional, you have many legitimate services to offer; interactions with colleagues will hopefully be respectful in both directions. If your client is seeing a primary-care therapist, you might seek permission to contact and collaborate with that person.

To convey your scope of practice to colleagues and clients, it may be useful to write up what you offer, perhaps in the form of a contract stating your responsibilities to your client and your client's responsibilities to you and the healing process you are undertaking together. Be aware, though, that even with the clearest of intentions, it is very easy to unconsciously collude with clients who want you to be their therapist. The trust and vulnerability given to good inner peace facilitators have many times seduced them into interactions that require skills beyond their ability. Be alert, and when you feel an "undertow" pulling you into confusion, be ready to take a deep breath, admit your limits, clarify boundaries, and provide a referral to a more appropriate healing arts professional if necessary.

Confidentiality

Whenever conversation with clients begins to move into a dynamic where I am playing the role of a counselor, I inform them that while I am not a trained psychotherapist and do not offer psychotherapy, they still may expect that I will observe appropriate professional ethics, especially concerning the confidentiality of anything said in the session. This by itself often opens the door to a deeper level of sharing. Here, though, is another scope of practice consideration: knowing myself, just how far can I *reasonably* guarantee that I won't unwittingly repeat confidential information?

For instance, referring to the session described at the beginning of this chapter, how might I respond if Susan's husband or one of her friends booked a session and, perhaps subtly, tried to get me to divulge what Susan had discussed with me? Would I "break under pressure"? Might I forget where I had learned a certain piece of information? If, under rigorous self-inspection, you conclude that "holding secrets" isn't your strong point, you might choose to discourage client disclosure of "delicate" information or, at the very least, avoid working with others who know your client. These aren't rules, but rather concerns a compassionate and ethical practitioner might do well to consider.

Source of Authority

In the discussion of healing versus curing in chapter 4, we considered the source of one's healing abilities. If healing power or wisdom is something that flows *through* us rather than something that originates *in* us, then imagining ourselves to be "authorities," meaning the author or source of what is happening, is simply an untruth that will interfere with the healing process. On the other hand, our role as healing arts professionals and inner peace facilitators requires that we set and maintain appropriate boundaries and offer guidance to clients who will naturally tend to see us as authority figures. Therefore, we are constantly challenged to discriminate between the legitimate and compassionate *use* of authority appropriate for the scope of our practice and the subtle, egocentric *abuse* of authority that harms our clients and, ultimately, ourselves.

It seems, then, that our task is to skillfully *play the role* our healing profession requires of us, while from moment to moment being receptive to guidance from the real source of all healing. We may be privileged to give our caring and offer ourselves as conduits for the healing process, but it is vital to remember that the authority that really counts is the Source, Spirit, or God.

The Practitioner as Role Model

Throughout this book there has been an emphasis on the importance of healing arts professionals actively working on melting the obstacles to *our own* inner peace. The old saying "Who we *are* speaks more loudly than what we *say*" is quite valid here. To the degree that we have reduced the obstacles to our own inner peace, *who we are* will be available as an inspiring example to our clients. Likewise, if our "vibes" are dissonant, unkind, and distracted, any wisdom coming through our mouths or hands will be received by our clients as part of a mixed message.

Therefore, remembering that "who we are is what we teach," many of us are deepening our commitment to draw forth and maintain our own inner truth, love, joy, freedom, and peace. As this process humbles us, we become softer, more accessible, more able to be touched by the wounded heart of a client longing to see living evidence that deep, meaningful healing really is possible.

The Practitioner as Educator

Our English word *educate* comes from the Latin *educere*, meaning to bring up, to lead, to draw forth. Implicit in this original definition is the idea that within each person is something of value to be led upward into consciousness. This is a very different concept from the one dominant in our culture today that suggests that education is about putting more facts and ideas *into* a mind rather than drawing forth what is already there.

In our culture's model, the teacher is an "authority," a source of information implicitly more valid than what is within the student. Originally, though, a teacher was seen as a skilled facilitator in a process of arousing curiosity, focusing motivation, and bringing into consciousness what the student already possessed within. The famous Socratic dialogues from ancient Greece embody this principle, as do current therapeutic offerings such as the "options process" and psychosynthesis.

Awareness of Transference and Countertransference

In psychotherapy training, students are taught the dynamics whereby clients unconsciously project their unresolved feelings from earlier people and situations onto people in the present ("transference"). One tipoff that this is happening is that the intensity of a client's reaction may not be totally appropriate to the current situation. As you have probably already learned, during bodywork sessions one can inadvertently access deep, often nonverbal, levels of emotion that can be quite confusing to both client and practitioner.

"Countertransference" refers to what happens when therapists project their unconscious, unresolved feelings onto a client and then react to them in ways inappropriate for a client-practitioner relationship. Both of these phenomena can easily sneak up on a practitioner; developing subtle awareness and appropriate response is a major part of a psychotherapist's training.

These phenomena can also be understood as the realm of the

"shadow," the unconscious part in each of us that because it is denied, builds up pressure and leaks out into the world and onto others. This is a fascinating realm for both intellectual study and personal exploration to support our growth as inner peace facilitators. It is also an area that can cause untold harm when misunderstood or repressed by a practitioner. Some supports that may be useful in this area include ongoing professional supervision, regular "clinic" sessions with other counseling bodyworkers, journal work, self-study, dream work, and quiet time to ponder our professional interactions.

Useful information for further exploration of transference and countertransference issues (as well as other aspects of psychotherapy) is found in the first few chapters of *Psychotherapy: The Art of Wooing Nature* by Sheldon Roth (a local college library may have a copy). For a delightful brief introduction to shadow work, see parts 2 and 3 of *A Little Book on the Human Shadow* by Robert Bly.

Containment and Appropriate Boundaries

As used here, *containment* refers to the cocreation by client and practitioner of a nurturing and respectful psychic space. In this safe, loving crucible, the client is helped to feel and explore the vulnerable inner world that usually includes old wounds, fears, anger, and denial. This healing relationship becomes a *conduit* that supports the client's evolution from habitual, constricting ways of being to those that are more authentic and embodied.

We must be aware, though, that this process can sometimes be frightening for a client. Therefore, it is important to progress slowly, gently yet firmly *containing* these long-suppressed energies as they come into consciousness. Our role as facilitator is to offer and maintain clear and appropriate boundaries that support our client in this work. This is a crucial skill for practitioners and also one that can take a tremendous amount of time and commitment to develop. Accurately appraising and honoring your current level of competence in this area is vitally important for clearly determining your scope of practice.

Client-Centered Session Time

There is a basic principle in this work that even the best of us may occasionally forget: Our clients have come to receive our attention and skilled assistance with *their* problems, not to hear about ours! So a useful question for each of us to ask inside before speaking in a client session might be, "Am I saying this for my client? Or for myself?"

When we are with friends, there is usually a give-and-take in the conversation; we are together with the understanding that both of us will get our needs met. However, in our professional role, the assumption is quite different. The client deals with our needs by paying us, not by listening as we gratify our desire to sound wise.

This is likewise valid for each decision we make regarding our clients. Am I suggesting a certain line of thinking for *their* benefit or because it currently happens to hold *my* interest? Am I using especially deep pressure at this moment because my perception of the healing process calls it forth or because I'm remembering anger at someone else and didn't notice that thought unconsciously intensifying my stroke? The questions keep getting subtler and subtler, which is why it is so important for practitioners to have our own ongoing practices for deepening awareness and heightening consciousness.

In addition, being a healing professional aware of what you can personally handle, you will probably want to develop a list of other professionals to whom you can refer clients when appropriate. As an ethical, client-centered practitioner, you will likely want to make referrals only to serve the interests of your client; discriminating between this principle and one's natural tendency to help one's friends through referrals may sometimes be a demanding challenge.

Dual Relationships

One issue that comes up for all of us sooner or later concerns multiple relationships with clients. While most ethical practitioners understand that sexual activity with a client is disruptive to maintaining a safe, therapeutic relationship, many of us may not have considered very deeply how adding other kinds of relationships may be confusing.

In counseling ethics, the term "dual relationship" refers to a situation in which the client-practitioner relationship is affected by one or more nontherapy relationships. The possibility of overlapping roles and the ensuing confusion as to appropriate behavior in each may well detract from the client's healing process since we have different sets of expectations and responses in each kind of relationship.

If, for instance, you have bartered with clients to pay for their sessions with you by cleaning your house, doing home repair work, or editing your writing, you must of necessity interact with them differently as an "employer" than you do as a healing arts professional. The compassion and focus on *their* needs that they have come to cherish and depend upon in their professional time with you may be strangely absent as you inform them how you want *your* oven cleaned, *your* window repaired, or *your* letter typed.

It is not impossible to keep dual roles separate and clearly defined, but there is a very high potential for disruption to an otherwise beneficial healing relationship. To explore this topic further, read "Dual Relationships and Other Ethical Considerations" in the spring 1992 issue of the *Massage Therapy Journal* (call AMTA at 708-864-0123 to order). Another excellent discussion is "The Duel Over Dual Relationships" by Michele Bograd in the November/December 1992 issue of *The Family Therapy Networker* (see resources in chapter 21).

Professional Supervision

As part of our continuing education, regular professional supervision is a powerful, personalized opportunity to both stretch your own inner limitations and also discuss any questions or problems you may be encountering with specific clients *without violating confidentiality*. A supervisor acts as a reliable "mirror" and is trained to help you see obscure or resistant parts of your inner makeup and deal with them consciously *before* they get you involved in countertransference and create client problems.

In all honesty, though, even with the best supervision, an occasional crisis with a client will arise. Perhaps there is a healing breakthrough that confuses both of you or an energy release that takes unexpected and disturbing directions. Without ongoing supervision, it is very tempting to try to minimize the problem or ignore it completely. In supervision, however, you can unravel and explore both the client's difficulties and your own limited and, perhaps, confused or frightened response to them.

An appropriate supervisor might be a psychotherapist, a senior practitioner of your modality, a spiritual guide, or a religious counselor. What is most important is that this person maintain the highest ethical standards, be familiar with the principles of your work, be skilled in psychodynamics, has done his or her own inner work to a deep level, and be an inspiring and competent role model for *your* evolution, just as you seek to be for your clients. (Please note that *legally* "professional supervision" might include responsibilities for the supervisor not discussed here, and it may therefore be necessary to adopt a different term for this relationship.) Another source of support could be an ongoing supervision group specifically focused on helping bodyworkers develop their counseling skills.

I feel a bit embarrassed as I write this section because for years I steadfastly refused to seek and pay for supervision, which I then believed was unnecessary. My own creativity was enough, I thought, and, besides, my inner guidance would provide all the wisdom I needed. Well, that all might be true in theory, but it ignores the simple fact that I do not always choose to *listen to* and *follow* my inner guidance—or may not be "awake" enough at the moment to do so!

In my case, an exceptionally challenging and potentially dangerous incident brought me to a place where paid professional supervision was "an offer I couldn't refuse." Now that I have been receiving supervision weekly for many years, I am convinced that this is a vital adjunct to the work of most healing arts professionals. And it is especially important to those of us evolving our skill and training through nontraditional means, where it is more likely that we may not have been exposed to some crucial element included in formal academic programs.

Another way to think of professional supervision is as a form of insurance. And it is a win-win policy: when your practice is not presenting problems, you can use your supervision time to deepen your personal awareness process; when difficulties with a client arise or you want to get clearer so they will not, you have an established, ongoing, supportive relationship in place and ready to serve you.

Yes, the mind may come up with all sorts of reasons why you cannot afford the cost on an ongoing basis. Yet if this cost were included as part of a required license to practice, most of us would somehow come up with it. The real issue, in my experience, is convincing myself that supervision is a *necessity,* not a *negotiable luxury.* Once that is done, the details of financing this tax-deductible business expense tend to work themselves out.

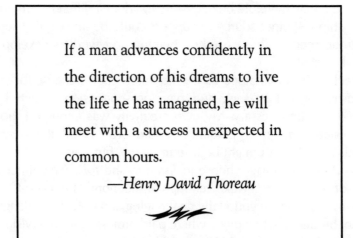

If a man advances confidently in
the direction of his dreams to live
the life he has imagined, he will
meet with a success unexpected in
common hours.

—*Henry David Thoreau*

Exploring Financial Accessibility in Your Practice

Cause, Effect, and Compassion

A major theme throughout this book has been that the most important thing we offer is *who we are*, not what we know or do. From this arises the understanding that the best "training" for facilitating inner peace in others is the practice of maintaining peace and contact with the center (or source of wisdom) within ourselves. One powerful approach to this process involves learning to observe our own inner *obstacles* to peace—moving past our habits of rationalization or denial into acceptance of what we observe. Then we can apply the "heat" of awareness and gradually melt these obstacles.

Peace is not something we can create. But like the emerging sun after the morning fog burns off, it will reveal itself as having always been with us when whatever was blocking it has dissolved. To the degree that this peace is shining unobstructed from our hearts, we are a welcoming environment in which others can pursue the release of their own inner light.

Peace as Harmony with Natural Law

A useful working definition of "peace" might be the use of our will (including thoughts, words, and deeds) in ways that are in harmony with what might be thought of as natural law, spiritual truth, or God's will. Patterns of thought and behavior that are not in harmony with these underlying principles are the obstacles that restrict access to the natural joy and peace that are our birthright.

195

For instance, many of us have linked arms and affirmed with all our hearts the knowledge that we are one. In moments of ecstatic clarity we may have directly experienced the unity of all life and the indescribable love that inevitably accompanies such realization. But soon our old ignorance reclaims our consciousness, and we continue in our illusion of separateness. Within this mental contraction, watching out for number one makes sense. Drawing to ourselves the ability to fulfill our desires seems so naturally right that it is rarely even questioned. Unfortunately, though, in this fog of constricted thinking, the "peace that passeth all understanding" remains only a dream.

The Law of Cause and Effect

In the spirit of a wake-up call, I invite you to consider the following: One of the most fundamental spiritual principles is the law of cause and effect. Every religion and culture expresses it in some way. "As you sow, so shall you reap" logically leads to "Do unto others as you would have others do unto you." This makes sense because the law says that sooner or later what you do will come back to you. Other approaches to this truth include "The macrocosm mirrors the microcosm," "As within, so without," and "You perceive only what you are." All express the underlying connection between that which "fate" brings to us and our thoughts, words, and deeds.

This principle implies that the universe is inherently a just place, that balance is fundamental to all aspects of existence, and that we each create our own future by how we use our free will in the present. The science of ecology studies these principles as they work through physical systems such as the flora and fauna of Earth. Systems theory and the working of feedback systems at every level of creation also illuminate this law.

What Is Wealth?

In light of this all-pervasive principle, let us now turn our attention to the deeper meaning of financial wealth. Money, of course, is a means of representing and exchanging that wealth. The classical economic definition of wealth is the ability to command (draw to yourself) goods and services. Since ultimately all goods are gifts from this planet plus someone's labor, all money actually represents some human being's time and energy.

Every time you spend money, you are actually "commanding" someone else to perform labor for you, regardless of how many levels of distance our economic system has created to disguise this fact. And most of the time we ignore the suffering caused by the injustice of the "bargain" exchange rates we as "haves" can impose on the "have nots." Here, the term *haves* applies to anyone, especially a healing arts professional, who has the power to dictate the terms of an exchange.

Anytime we use our will to get another to serve us, anytime the fulfillment of desire engages the labor (through money) of another, we are entering into an exchange process. We may have our opinions as to its fairness, but mostly we are ignorant of how the law of cause and effect will perceive its balance. If, for instance, as a bodywork practitioner I require $50 for an hour of my time, and if you are able to command only $5 per hour for yours, then I am requiring that you give me ten hours of your labor for one hour of mine. If the discomfort from your muscle tension is intense enough, you may even consider this a good deal. As human societies, we have created all sorts of rationalizations to justify such exchanges. But how sure are we that the underlying law of balance will agree with us?

Balancing Valuations in Client Financial Exchanges

For those who have become humble and truthful enough to see that our own valuations *may* be out of harmony with deeper underlying principles, enlightened self-interest suggests that we try to minimize imbalance in all of our energy transactions. How to do that, though, will boggle the mind if *thought* is the only instrument used to address the problem. "My massage is *worth* $50" is a thought, for example; "I need $40,000 a year to survive" is another thought.

If such thoughts are in harmony with the underlying principles governing your life, they should not interfere with your inner peace. Since (for most of us) thoughts of worth, value, money, and fulfillment of desire *do* disturb our inner peace, we might consider looking for a deeper source of wisdom and guidance than the mind can offer.

If there is a higher power operating in your life, accessing its wisdom offers a way through the confusion and contradictions of mind. In each situation our spirit, guardian angel, God, or highest truth *knows* what decisions will bring the greatest benefit to all and create the least potential for future suffering. What is necessary to access this wisdom is a willingness to quiet the mind, listen through the silence with an open heart, and humbly follow the guidance we are offered.

Fees as Gatekeeper

One crucial question that confronts each healing arts practitioner is deciding with whom we will work. Most of us use our society's default answer: If you can afford my fee, welcome; if not, forget it. We allow money to be a major "gatekeeper" for our services. Since money allows us to fulfill many of our desires, we rarely consider whether using it as a gatekeeper is supportive or detrimental to our long-term well-being.

Just as the law of cause and effect makes us indebted in imbalanced transactions, so does it also generate mercy and grace in the wake of our selfless offering of service and compassion for others. The more we become conscious of how painful it is to endure the "effects" of *our own* past unconscious deeds—and the healing that eventually frees us from them—the more we can directly experience how sweet and how necessary compassion is for *anyone's* healing process.

The Value of Compassion

One practical definition of compassion is that it is the freely offered "grease" that lubricates the incessant grinding away of the mechanism of cause and effect in our lives. Since our evolution and healing are so greatly nurtured by this balm, and since each of us can see how receiving compassion has made our own roads easier to travel, we might wish to offer it to others when the painful effects of their previous decisions leaves them weak and in need of a service we can provide. As we give freely to others, we open wide the doors to receiving freely from that universal compassion that ultimately sustains us all.

Compassion, like inner peace, must first shine within if we are to realize the fullest unfolding of our healing potential. Compassion for oneself, though, can easily be confused with complacency, in which we notice the causes of our suffering and forgive ourselves but do little to change them. While genuine self- compassion definitely contains acceptance and forgiveness, it *also* entails a rigorous commitment to *change* the thoughts and behaviors that cause suffering for both others and ourselves. Though challenging—and at times painfully difficult—

when we are devoted to truth and compassion as we examine our beliefs and habits, the harmony and peace that radiate from this process become a blessing to each person we are privileged to serve.

Spiritual Capitalism

I like to think of this approach to service as a form of "Spiritual Venture Capitalism." In the marketplace form of venture capitalism, investors put money into a business with the expectation that a lot more money will be returned to them. In spiritual venture capitalism, the investment is not money so much as time, energy, thought, caring, and love. The payoff comes as wounded humans find their way to healing— as the bud of potential within each of us is nurtured and coaxed to unfold its magnificent flower that has been lying dormant within. As all life rejoices in the release of this beauty, so, too, must our lives be enriched and blessed.

Financial Accessibility Considerations

What Does Being Financially Accessible Really Mean?

Fundamentally, being "financially accessible" means inviting clients to discuss their financial situation with you along with all of the other issues that affect your healing relationship. It is part of a holistic practice, one of many factors that influence our ability to be effective as healing arts professionals.

Being financially accessible does not necessarily mean that you agree to work with all people regardless of their ability to pay. It does mean, however, that you are willing to consider a wide variety of factors in choosing whether to develop a healing relationship with a particular person. These factors may include the client's ability to pay, your current financial situation, and the pressure on your time at present.

In other words, being financially accessible means that you choose not to use a set fee as the primary "gatekeeper" for determining who has access to your services. After making this decision, a wide variety of possibilities open up. Organizations such as the Guild of (financially) Accessible Practitioners (see last part of this appendix) exist so that we might share these possibilities with each other and learn how they are working in actual practice.

What Financial Accessibility Can Mean for You

A primary motivation for many healing arts professionals to be financially accessible is the joy of working with motivated, sincere clients whose readiness to benefit from our work is our number one reason for seeing them. Along with this comes an enhanced sense of personal and professional integrity in knowing that we are first of all healing arts professionals and not just merchants who "sell" time slots. In addition to the sense of well-being and inner peace this can bring, it may also draw clients to our practice who are delightful to work with, ready to heal, and—because of the availability of our service—become freer and more energetic in their service to others.

For those of us who feel that our healing abilities flow, at least in some part, from a higher power, practicing financial accessibility means including that higher power in the decision of who our clients are. Letting potential clients know that paying a set fee is not a rigid requirement for seeing us allows many other factors to come into play that might otherwise have remained hidden.

A Few Reasons for Exploring Financial Accessibility

Most of us are probably influenced to a greater or lesser degree by each of the following motivations, and the list is hardly complete. You might notice whether you agree or disagree with, feel attracted to or repelled by each of these motivating factors; they are offered as tools to help clarify thinking and values. Feel free to add others to the list.

1. **Spirit as Source:** Since I understand that God is the ultimate source of all healing, I seek to be as much as possible a willing conduit for serving those whom the Source brings my way.

2. **Recognition of oneness (compassion):** One spirit exists in all of us. Hence, any denial of healing to the spirit embodied in another is a denial of healing to oneself. From this view, all service to another is really service to oneself—to the one spirit as it seeks freedom in another's form. Because of my compassion for "my" spirit's suffering in *any* form, to deny service to another hurts me more than the possible results of a lower income.

3. **Justice:** Our society's norms concerning financial accessibility are unjust and contribute to the pain and suffering in the world.

Pursuit of greater justice in financial relationships with clients is seen as an integral part of other political, social, and economic beliefs.

4. **Voluntary simplicity:** "I choose to live simply so that others may simply live." Financial accessibility is an outgrowth of personal lifestyle choices that reduce the need and desire for larger incomes. Offering of professional skills is more for its own sake than as a means of providing income to support one's lifestyle. Included here might also be the recognition that the future may bring leaner times economically, and thus there is a desire to prepare for living happily with reduced income voluntarily now rather than waiting and being forced to do so later.

5. **Charity and/or guilt:** I have so much that I owe something to others who have less (noblesse oblige). This recognition may include doing something to ease my conscience.

6. **As an inadvertent result of income-maximizing strategy:** A practitioner might decide, for instance, to offer "standby" sessions at half price to clients able to come on very short notice in the event of a last-minute vacancy. Other possibilities might include reduced fees for a series of sessions or for prepaid sessions, for referrals to friends, and so on.

Various Policies for Determining Client Fees

The following are several fee policies in use by healing arts practitioners. Which have you tried? Which have worked well in your experience?

1. **Fixed fee, non-negotiable.** The cost per session is published, and any client making an appointment assumes responsibility for paying the full amount.

2. **Fixed fee, negotiable.** The cost per session is published with an option that clients may request a fee reduction in cases where the set fee is not possible or creates extreme hardship. *Responsibility is on the client to seek an exemption.*

3. **Sliding scale, practitioner determined.** A sliding scale of fees is published by the practitioner. The client's income and perhaps other financial factors are discussed, and a session fee is deter-

mined and mutually accepted. Discussions may be reopened from time to time or when the client's financial situation changes.

4. **Sliding scale, honor system.** This is essentially the same as above, but the client determines the fee to be paid using the sliding scale without discussing or needing approval from the practitioner.

5. **Client-determined fee with a suggested range.** The client is solely responsible for determining the amount appropriate for each session's fee. A suggested range is provided as a reference for comparable value of service in the marketplace, but it is offered for guidance only.

6. **Client-determined fee, contribution, or donation with no guidance offered.** Phrases such as "Whatever you offer is fine" or "Please pay as much as is appropriate for your financial situation" are the only guidance to the client in determining what to pay for a session.

7. **Barter arrangements** for all or part of the above. Amounts, responsibilities, and terms are negotiated between provider and client. This is a "dual relationship" and has possible difficulties, as well as benefits, for each party.

8. **Pro bono, charity, and other gifts of services.** The practitioner provides accessibility outside of the regular practice. Possible ways include donating time at a clinic or other service facility, at a residence for disadvantaged persons, or at an outreach project of a charitable organization.

With numbers 2 through 7 above, a practitioner might choose to place limits on the number of clients accepted in order to leave enough time for higher-paying clients. Also, each of the above can be explicit, publicized policies (proactive) or decided case by case according to need (reactive).

Considering the Relative Worth of the Client's and Practitioner's Time

In the book *Your Money or Your Life* by Vickie Robin and Joe Dominguez, there is a useful chapter explaining how to calculate the actual cost of things you acquire in terms of the work hours of your life you have exchanged to get them. Also, there is guidance for computing your realistic income per hour taking into account *all* of your "earning costs."

For instance, let us say you bill $50 per hour for your time. After factoring in the costs of doing business, the time spent maintaining your professional skills, taking care of your office, and unbillable phone time with clients, you may actually net only $10 or $15 per hour. Likewise, when a client who earns $10 per hour adjusts her or his hourly income to account for travel time, clothing costs, eating out, and postwork recuperation, the person may actually be making a net income of only $4 or $5 per hour.

With the use of these more realistic figures, it becomes apparent how our fee structure expresses our beliefs about the relative value of practitioner and client time. For example, if my net income is $15 per hour and a certain client's net income is $3 per hour, then our work-hours exchange rate is five to one. Consciously or unconsciously I am agreeing to exchange the "fruits" of one hour of my time for the "fruits" of five hours of my client's time. Likewise, if Client B earns a net of $30 per hour, I am exchanging one hour of my work time for a half hour of her work time.

Such inequalities in exchange rates are so pervasive in our culture that most of us hardly think about them. Charging "what the market will bear" is almost a religion with many practitioners, yet how often do we consider the fundamental beliefs upon which this custom is based?

So, for starters, perhaps you might ask yourself how large a ratio of practitioner-to-client net earnings you feel comfortable with. For instance, if I ask from one to four times as much from my client in net work hours as I give back, that might feel within reason. Does five times as much feel OK? Ten times? Or, to put it another way, I may feel all right exchanging an hour of my time for what my client can earn in half a day. When I find myself requiring that a client pay an entire day's net income in exchange for an hour of my time, though, perhaps I might feel that this is too much, even if the actual dollar amount is very reasonable compared to what other practitioners charge.

When you have discovered what ratio feels appropriate for your values, try to guess how many hours net income your least-affluent clients give you in exchange for your time. Do the exchange-rate numbers that are created by your fee structure feel appropriate to you now?

Fears and Realities

Many practitioners experience fears concerning what might happen if they sincerely attempt to make their practice more financially accessible. Following are a few common ones and the realities that might accompany them.

Fear: I will be inundated with poor clients and go bankrupt.

Reality: Becoming *more* financially accessible does not necessarily mean that you relinquish all say concerning client fees. Remember, to be accessible at all, you must *be there*. This necessitates paying the rent, eating, meeting utility bills, and all of the other financial necessities that are part of providing your professional service.

Each successful practitioner finds a workable balance between lower-paying and higher-paying clients. At times, remaining financially accessible *in general* may mean limiting time available to lower-paying clients and actively seeking those whose financial resources can help you meet your monetary needs.

Fear: I won't get what I need.

Reality: Most of us who have grown up in this culture have absorbed a great deal of confusion concerning the difference between needs and desires. Things that are commonly considered "needs" by many of us are seen as great luxuries by the vast majority of the world's people.

To the degree that we feel committed to serving those who are well-matched for what we offer professionally, *independent of what they can provide for us financially,* we may find ourselves reexamining our beliefs concerning the dividing line between needs and desires. We might choose to experiment and find out whether, indeed, all we *truly* need will be provided for us. We might try letting the natural ebb and flow of financial wealth determine what "extras" we get and when.

Fear: If I don't stand up for myself and ask for what I know I'm worth, I won't get what I deserve in life.

Reality: Genuine healing arts professionals generally do not get what they are truly worth—there just is not enough money available for that! Our culture's adoption of fixed price structures reflects the commoditization of healing, not its inherent worth. A commodity can be *valued*—that is, it can have a price on it relative to similar commodities in the market place. *Worth*, however, is a quality inherent in something, independent of its relative financial *value*. (Check it out in the dictionary.)

The idea of *deserving* something is another tricky concept that bears investigation. When dealing with pricing structures, *deserving* is a relative concept: Do I *deserve* an extra $20 from my client more than my client's children *deserve* a new pair of shoes? Do I *deserve* the lifestyle accompanying a $35,000 per year income more than some of my clients *deserve* to live without fear of having their electricity cut off or not being able to pay their rent? By what *values* do I answer such questions? How much integrity do I bring to applying these values to *every* aspect of my life?

Fear: I'm afraid I'll feel resentful and bitter if I don't get a certain amount of the good things in life.

Reality: Of course we want an abundance of the goodness life has to offer—that's healthy! And by some definitions, part of our duty as health professionals is to be a shining example of radiant health.

The question for us to grapple with in this case is, What is our inner programming concerning the nature of abundance? If we define it largely as things and services requiring payment in money, then the above fear is indeed realistic. However, if our feelings of abundance arise more from an inner sense of well-being, from feeling cared for and taken care of by life, and from having learned to love and share freely and joyously, then money—and how much we receive from a given client—is of relatively minor importance in our experiencing an abundant life.

Exploring this fear invites us to look at some bigger questions: What is the true source of all abundance? Where does the joy we seek in life really come from? Upon what do we place our faith for getting what we truly need? The money clients hand us at the end of a session may *appear* to be the source of our support, but what lies behind its flow? What does it do to the totality of that flow to refuse to work with someone simply because that person appears not to be able to give us enough money?

Fear: If I set my fees too low, people will assume my service is not worth much.

Reality: Being financially accessible does not necessarily mean advertising a low fee. It does mean, though, that you let clients know that you are open to dealing with everything in their unique situations, including the financial aspects, and developing a treatment plan that is workable and satisfying for both of you.

Fear: I'm afraid of being taken advantage of by clients who can afford to pay more but are stingy.

Reality: It is true that sometimes you may feel ripped off. However, by developing your intuition, your interviewing skills, and your courage to ask for what you believe is right in each situation, you can limit such instances to a very small percentage of your practice. When inevitably a "cheater" does slip by, you might comfort yourself with the old adage "If you're not making any mistakes, you're not taking any risks." And if you're not taking any risks, how can you grow?

When Clients Are Scarce

Throughout more than a decade of supporting myself as a healing arts practitioner, I have noticed cycles of plenty and cycles of "drought." In the times of plenty, the economic strategy is easy: give all of your clients your best, and they will return as well as tell their friends. Once you get established, promotion can become a very minor concern.

But in drought times, when because of its silence you wonder whether your phone line has been cut or when you are new to an area or just starting out, that is when there is a need to hustle. Yet advertising, the traditional response, is least accessible because you do not have the income to pay for it. In times like this, I find that my number-one priority needs to be to keep working—keep my healing talents flowing regardless of how much I might or might not get paid for my effort.

Perhaps there is a local charity you would like to support. Send them a write-up describing what you offer and a "gift certificate" (official or hand drawn) for a complimentary session for the worker currently most in need of appreciation and support. You will feel good, you will probably get tremendous appreciation from whomever was selected to receive your gift, and perhaps they will tell their friends and associates. They may even come back eventually as a paying client.

One concern many practitioners have is that if they agree to see a lower-paying client in a certain time slot, then they may end up having to turn away a higher-paying one. If this is a realistic concern for you, why not offer a "standby" rate of, perhaps, half of your normal fee for clients able to show up on short notice. You might also accept tentative requests for appointments at a certain time, subject to confirmation the day before (or the morning of the session) *if* the time period remains unfilled. This lets you attempt to steer bookings to other time periods, but also leaves you free to let a higher-paying client "bump" a lesser-paying one in the event that no other option works out.

When you describe this kind of arrangement to your lesser-paying clients, you might want to go out of your way to let them know that you in no way consider them inferior to higher-paying ones and that the service and attention they will receive when with you will be identical. However, their ability to be flexible on scheduling allows you to pick up an extra session, and you want to show your appreciation by accommodating their need to pay less. If you get really skillful at this, you may even leave the lesser-paying clients feeling they have done *you* a favor with their flexibility!

Peacefully Accepting Feeling "Taken Advantage Of"

Another important skill to develop is appraising whether clients actually need a price break to be able to come to you or whether they are just being stingy. However, though I have been practicing healing arts for more than twenty-five years, I must confess that life still has not revealed to me a foolproof way to do this. What I have learned, though, is that some small percentage of the time I am going to guess wrong and end up feeling ripped off. My task, then, is to accept that this just "goes with the territory": if I am going to attempt to fully live my values of compassion by offering financial accessibility, sometimes I may be taken advantage of.

I try to think of what I am doing as analogous to one of the principles of organic farming. In that approach, while you try to cut crop loss by a variety of nontoxic methods, you still must accept that a certain percentage of your food will be lost to pests. So you decide that, for instance, a 5 percent loss is acceptable. You do what you can to maximize your yield, but you also are content if losses stay below 5 percent. This is a path of health for the soil and environment, and a path of mental health for the farmer. And after several years, the farmer may even discover that allowing these losses (and not spending extra money on excessive pest controls) has actually *increased* the year's income!

Likewise, I could try to eliminate those reduced-fee clients who might easily afford more, but who I feel are taking advantage of me (pests). In the process, though, I will probably turn away some appropriate low-fee people and possibly also end up creating a toxic mindset for myself. Even a profit-driven commercial store would be satisfied with a low shoplifting rate; if it can live with such losses, so can I.

There are additional ways to make your services more financially accessible. One approach is to link what clients pay with how much they support and promote your work. So, for instance, you can have a "buy three, get one free" offer that effectively gives clients a 25 percent discount while giving you three times more income than from only one session. You might also have a policy that for every two or three referred clients who book a session, your regular clients receive one complimentary session. If they are industrious and skillful, they might never have to pay for a session again, while you may be looking at a full practice with very little promotional expense.

Success Breeds Success

The underlying principle behind all of these ideas is that success breeds success, and movement tends to continue moving. If you can keep your healing abilities flowing in committed service to those whose needs are appropriate for what you offer, it is my experience that the universe does its part and provides you with the necessary finances to continue. The word *necessary* is key here, and other discussions both in this book and with colleagues, counselors, and friends will hopefully help in the process of understanding what this means in *your* life.

One thing that repeatedly saddens me is the bumper sticker (and the mentality behind it) that says, "He who dies with the most toys wins." In addition to revealing values of extreme materialism and selfishness, it evokes the image of a millionaire in a room surrounded by every goody imaginable, alone, lonely, and confused as death exacts its inevitable due. In response to this vision, I imagine a bumper sticker that reads, "She who shares the most joys wins."

We who have been blessed with healing abilities have more than toys to give away—we have an opportunity to be instruments through which clients reconnect with their innate sense of health, vitality, balance, and peace. We have an opportunity many times each day to be midwives to the birthing of new life out of old dis-ease. From *this* derives our wealth. Financial affluence may come to some and not to others, may visit you during one period of your life, yet abandon you during another. But always, if the yearning to serve is strong and true, I have found there is "enough." Call it faith, call it foolish wisdom, but the Master Healer will not allow a willing servant to go uncared for.

About the Guild of (financially) Accessible Practitioners

In this time of rapid change and economic uncertainty, many healing arts professionals are becoming more interested in examining their ideas and policies concerning client financial accessibility. Many are also attempting to apply more fully their ideals of personal integrity, their beliefs about social and economic justice, and their spiritual awareness to *all* of the various aspects of their professional practice. In an age dominated by materialistic values, this can often be a lonely and frustrating challenge.

To nurture this growing link between one's deepest principles and client work, the Guild of (financially) Accessible Practitioners was created in 1993. The Guild is a broad-based network that welcomes all practitioners of the healing arts who either have been or wish to explore the possibility of making a substantial part of their professional services available to those who need them independent of the client's ability to pay.

The Guild is an ongoing forum for grappling with emotion-laden questions concerning money, prosperity, personal and political values, respect, and financial accessibility. Through a quarterly newsletter, the semiannual *Financial Accessibility Journal,* local support groups, and other direct connections, we share support, clarity, and courage to "walk our talk" more fully. The Guild espouses no particular policies, but instead offers a wide range of approaches for considering these issues and a means for sharing successes and difficulties.

Some practitioners seek greater financial accessibility in their practice because of their political principles and beliefs concerning social and economic justice and public policy. Others, motivated by their spiritual beliefs, are struggling to understand and clarify the relationship between God (or inner spirit), their particular healing talents, and those with whom we share these talents professionally. There are also practitioners who feel compelled by their hearts to alleviate suffering unconditionally when presented with the opportunity, yet have conflicts about this as they consider economic and other aspects of their lives.

Regardless of motivation, sincere investigation of financial accessibility issues often leads to questions such as "What are viable alternatives?" and "What is currently working for other practitioners?" The Guild exists to encourage and support the exploration of many of the topics discussed in this book including:

❖ The practice of "living simply that others may simply live."
❖ Discriminating more clearly between needs and desires.
❖ Becoming clear on valuing what is offered professionally, independent of the amount of money received for it.
❖ Dealing with feelings of "being taken advantage of" and other emotions that may arise in relation to our dominant materialistic culture.

The vision for the Guild grew over several years, officially coming into existence at the beginning of a season of light, December 21, 1993. By its second year there were more than a hundred members representing a broad range of healing professions. Guild publications offer articles, letters from practitioners, information on local chapters, book and article summaries, reasons for exploring financial accessibility, various fee policies used by practitioners, and ways to consider the relative worth of client and practitioner time. They also include information about each member so as to facilitate communication.

One of the Guild's major goals is to produce a comprehensive handbook discussing the wide variety of topics influencing how a practitioner determines fees and financial accessibility. Some issues to be explored include clarifying personal and professional values and beliefs, understanding how practitioners and clients value services offered, feelings about using money as a "gatekeeper" to one's practice, handling conflicts and ambivalence in values, needs versus desires, how much is enough, and spiritual entrepreneurship. The Guild plans to make this handbook available in an attractive, low-cost edition to all healing arts schools for distribution and use in their business classes.

There are two complementary levels of participation in the Guild. On the local level, members meet face-to-face and share what is working for them financially, what is not working, their fears, and their visions. Chapters have the option of forming local referral networks for their members, creating interdisciplinary provider programs, and offering client and practitioner education. Chapters can also be formed within a professional association to address the needs of a specific profession.

Nationally, the Guild collects and distributes information among members and local groups to increase awareness of various possibilities and resources. It also provides information to other groups and publications, many of which are entering into similar explorations as personal and professional integrity—and issues of accessibility to health and healing—become a growing public concern. Eventually the Guild will be accessible online, allowing practitioners all over the world to exchange information and participate in ongoing electronic dialogues concerning their specific situations and needs.

An excellent introduction to the Guild of (financially) Accessible Practitioners and the variety of ideas shared in its publications is the Guild's first book, *Financial Accessibility Issues and Answers*. Issues of the *Financial Accessibility Journal* are also available. In addition, anyone interested may request quantities of the Guild brochure for sharing with colleagues and building interest in forming a local Guild chapter.

The only requirements for Guild membership are an interest in exploring financial accessibility issues and help in paying the operating costs. As of early 1996, yearly dues were $35. In keeping with the principle of being financially accessible, smaller amounts are also accepted if necessary.

For further information, please call (888) 2-THE GAP.

* * *

The following article, "Client-Determined-Fee Experiment Works," *is reprinted from* Financial Accessibility Issues and Answers. *This article's appearance in several magazines drew a great deal of interest and was instrumental in creating the momentum for starting the Guild of (financially) Accessible Practitioners.*

A counselor and bodywork practitioner near Boston has been experimenting with inviting clients to determine their own session fees. After four years of having a fixed fee (and offering reductions to low-income clients if asked), he changed his financial policy in 1989. He then revised his publicity to include the line: **The session fee is determined by you.**

When prospective clients called, they were sent a brochure that explained his spiritually oriented bodywork in detail and included the following financial information:

> An amount in the range of $50-75 is suggested in most situations. **However,** if you have more limited finances and feel that this experience would be beneficial for you, whatever you offer will be joyfully accepted.

When asked why he operates this way, the practitioner explained, "Whatever skills I can offer come from a higher power. For me it's God, but I have no attachment to specific words or dogmas.

"There is a picture where I work of the blue Earth suspended in the black void of space, and I try to talk of her when appropriate and point out the need for each of us to do whatever we can to help humanity wake up and stop harming her. If through these sessions people can relax more deeply and see themselves more clearly, then hopefully they will also discover the will to live more harmoniously with each other and the Earth.

"The usual cost for sessions like this can sometimes be a barrier for a person who is otherwise ready to work on melting their inner obstacles to deeper awareness and peace. Therefore, each client is invited to determine her or his own fee. Some are exceedingly generous, and others may offer something more modest."

In analyzing his records over the past eight years, the practitioner discovered that the *average* fee for all client sessions has remained about the same, while his business volume has grown substantially, thereby increasing his total income. Even though he now gets many more low-income clients paying in the $20 to $30 range, he also gets enough in the $60 to $75 range to keep the overall session average at just about $50. And by operating this way, he avoids having to make the uncomfortable judgment of who qualifies for reduced fees.

Client Education

A Sample Brochure

The following are pages excerpted from a sixteen-page booklet I developed in 1993 to send to prospective clients. After a year of use, experience suggested that it probably presented too much material for an introductory brochure. It proved to be an excellent "filter," drawing clients who were highly motivated to participate in what was being offered. It also appears, however, to have filtered out others who may have been overwhelmed with it all. So in the fall of 1994 I returned to distributing a simple three-fold brochure to most inquiries (with the story in chapter 1 tucked inside), saving the full booklet for persons expressing special interest in the "Melting the Obstacles to Inner Peace" theme.

You are invited to take whatever ideas might be useful from these pages and incorporate them into your own brochure. Please feel free to contact me if you would like to brainstorm about how you might present your own unique offerings to potential clients.

Please note: The article listed in the brochure's table of contents as being on pages 9 through 12 appears in expanded form as chapter 2 of this book. The information in "About Your Facilitator" appears in expanded form as "About the Author" at the end of this book.

213

Melting the Obstacles
to
Inner Peace

Each three-hour session
integrates transformation-oriented bodywork
with insightful dialogue investigating the
personal and spiritual issues affecting
your own unique growth process

An excellent complement to other healing processes and therapies

Compassionate Midwifery For Emerging Peace

FROM STEPPINGSTONE

Melting the Obstacles to Inner Peace is a retreat to an island in time

In this spacious, safe environment we collaborate to reveal, soften, and melt the obstacles currently keeping you from enjoying your birthright of Freedom, Love, Joy, Truth, and Peace. Dan's role as an inner peace facilitator in both the verbal and hands-on work is to be a "midwife" for these gifts of the spirit gestating within you. Visions of joy and awareness of old inner pain intermingle as each session investigates and explores constricting assumptions and habits of mind, body, emotion, and spirit.

In this work spiritual investigation refers to a very practical, well reasoned approach to harmonizing conflicts of body, mind, and emotion. As context, we draw forth an integrating vision of your life's higher purpose and your own next step toward its fulfillment. Spirit is your inner truth, your higher Self; Its gifts are your birthright. Throughout all the drama of our lives, It is calm, It Knows. The Spirit within subtly guides us, if we would but hear and follow. It is Spirit that tugs at our heart and evokes a yearning for Home.

Spirit is that part of us that remembers expansiveness and longs for Freedom beyond anything political or social struggle can ever offer. Spirit is Love, but a vastly more encompassing Love then a few rewarding personal relationships. Spirit is Joy, yearning to take consciousness beyond any limited pleasure of the senses. Spirit is Truth, itching to transcend the confusion and artificial ignorance of mundane thinking, longing to See with Light unfiltered by mental distortion or emotional blockage. And Spirit is Peace, the Peace that passeth all understanding, the Peace having which, I have everything.

— 2 —

Topics for Investigation

Steppingstone sessions support you in unfolding and honoring the wisdom of your own unique Spirit. Using its guidance, we work together to uncover and heal those wounded places inside which are limiting the full and joyful expression of your natural gifts. This collaboration offers you an opportunity to integrate both verbal and physical ways of exploring various areas of your life, including:

• *Integrating your spiritual beliefs and principles into your daily life.*

• *Clarifying your own unique sense of "spirit."*

• *Conflicts between what you actually believe, and unconsciously absorbed values which interfere with your decision-making process.*

• *Finding the courage to uncover and continue healing the hidden painful places within.*

• *Working with the great spiritual questions, such as, "Who am I?" and the central organizing questions such as, "What is the purpose of my life?"*

• *Exploring your "shadow" self,*

learning how it projects out unconsciously, creating suffering for yourself and others. This might include inner child, childhood abuse, and recovery issues.

• *Dealing with "dry" times in your therapeutic or spiritual practices.*

• *Reframing current problems to reveal more creative solutions.*

• *The richness (or lack thereof) in your current relationship with your higher power.*

• *Your relationship with your body (chronic tension patterns, constricted breathing, restricted sensory awareness).*

• *Relationships with others.*

Contents

Your First Steppingstone Session

At the beginning of your *Steppingstone* session there is time to unwind and get acquainted over a cup of tea. Only one or two people are seen each day, so there is abundant time and energy available for you. The environment is a quiet home on a peaceful tree-lined street, a retreat apart and special.

Generally we will spend 1 - 1½ hours talking together, ending this part of the session by developing a clear focus for the coming bodywork. During the next 1 - 1½ hours, skilled hands draw into consciousness the physical aspects of the issues we've been exploring verbally. In this collaboration, the bodywork unfolds through continuous interaction with your tension patterns, your feedback, and your own unique ways of processing emotions which may arise.

Awareness of your breath is an ongoing focus in this work, guiding you to the realization that deep, regular breathing is intimately related to your sense of empowerment and ability to process difficult information skillfully. The strokes are firm and sensitive, coaxing you to relax into opening. The work moves slowly into deeper layers of blocked energy and tension, occasionally touching inner reservoirs of blocked pain. You retain control, though, and the pain is never more than you choose to deal with at that moment.

Steppingstone sessions offer you insightful tools for experiencing yourself in ways not normally available. Healing hands guide your consciousness and become a mirror through which you can *see* the subtle flows, blockages, and armoring which define and create

---

If peace of mind is your goal,
   look for errors in your beliefs and expectations.
Seek to change them, and not the world.
   - And always be prepared to be wrong.

But if being right is your goal,
   you will find the error in the world,
and seek to change it.
   - But don't ever expect peace of mind.

Peter Russell, author of *The Global Brain*
and *A White Hole in Time*

Steppingstone sessions help you find peace of mind

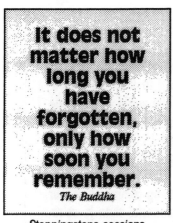

It does not matter how long you have forgotten, only how soon you remember.

The Buddha

Steppingstone sessions help you remember

who you are. As your inner awareness grows, as the energy patterns within change, *you* change. When the vehicle in which you live becomes more alive and less bound by old limitations, your consciousness expands. And this can lead to a wonderfully renewing and empowering vision of possibilities for yourself and for our lives together here with our Mother Earth.

After the bodywork, there is time available before you leave for exploring and integrating the subtle feelings and expanded awareness which may have come to the surface. Possible ways of doing this include meditating, writing, talking, or just being alone for awhile. You may also wish to do some yoga or other stretching, enjoying the new expansiveness and freedom in your body. Whatever you decide, this extra time is an opportunity to appreciate the precious gift you have given yourself, and to come into a deeper relationship with your newly discovered aliveness and inner peace.

Continuing the Work

The first session is an introduction, a getting-to-know each other. In succeeding sessions the work becomes more focused, able to move gradually beyond superficial tightness, down through the various layers of limitation and chronic tension accumulated over a lifetime. As our work together evolves, you learn to become more skillful in receiving exactly what your body needs, creating in your special retreat time the most relaxing and freeing experience possible.

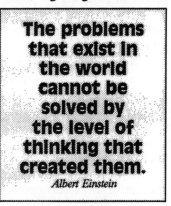

The problems that exist in the world cannot be solved by the level of thinking that created them.

Albert Einstein

Steppingstone sessions expand consciousness

> Those of us who have been on a spiritual path of consciousness know how it works. We know that when we make some changes internally they are immediately reflected in our life. Everything shifts. We need to understand how powerful that is. We really do affect the world – each one of us – when we do that transformational process in ourselves. That's really the most powerful effect we can have on the world. Then we can do things like taking political and social action. Those things are important. But if we take external action on the basis of being committed to our own growth process, it's much more powerful than if we're just projecting the problem outside of ourselves. We need to understand that our society is a reflection of consciousness. As our consciousness changes, our experience of life shifts.
> *Shakti Gawain*

Steppingstone sessions help you see life differently

Three Approaches to Bodywork

The field of professional bodywork and massage has three major approaches or orientations. Each has a particular model of reality, focus, goal, and purpose.

• *The medical/remedial orientation* views this work as part of the medical model of illness and is generally designed to "cure" bothersome symptoms.

• *The relaxation/recreation orientation* focuses on enjoyment, sensual pleasure, and temporary relief from muscle tension.

• *The transformation orientation* may include aspects of the above, but primarily seeks to support long-term change in consciousness, physical structure, energy use, and other habit patterns. It focuses less on temporary "cures" than on revealing and releasing the *cause* of the dis-ease, opening the door to true healing.

The work offered at *Steppingstone* is one of many effective transformation-oriented approaches. *Steppingstone does not offer medical/remedial services;* referrals to other practitioners are available as needed.

Curing versus Healing

It is common to confuse suppressing a symptom with healing the cause of that symptom. For instance, if you take an aspirin to reduce the pain of a headache, you may be curing the symptom called "headache," but this does nothing to affect the underlying cause of the dis-ease. The word "disease" here is intentionally divided as a reminder that painful symptoms are usually warnings that something is out of balance inside, that somehow we have lost our natural "ease" in living. Turning off this warning message may only set the stage for the inner physician to seek our cooperation with ever more "attention getting" symptoms.

Healing, in contrast to curing, is an act of will, even if that act is only to cease resisting, let go, and allow healing energy to enter and perform its work inside. Healing, in other words, requires cooperation. Curing can happen *to* you; healing must in some way be invited and accepted *by* you.

Steppingstone sessions offer an opportunity to deepen your personal healing process and see more clearly and compassionately the dis-ease existing inside you. Within the session's safe, supportive environment, your own dormant healing potential is drawn forth and focused to transform old, constricting inner wounds into flowing, creative vital energy for serving your life's highest purpose.

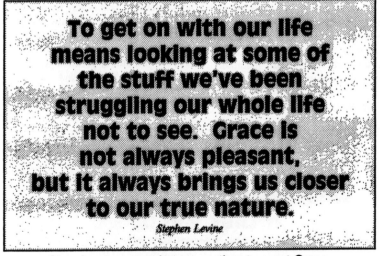

To get on with our life
means looking at some of
the stuff we've been
struggling our whole life
not to see. Grace is
not always pleasant,
but it always brings us closer
to our true nature.

Stephen Levine

Steppingstone sessions are a time to court Grace

Questions and Answers

Q: Is *Steppingstone's* inner peace facilitation similar to psychotherapy?
A: While *Steppingstone* does not offer academically credentialed psychotherapy, you may expect:

• compassionate guidance rooted in contemporary psychological understanding and time-tested spiritual principles.

• intuitive, empathetic attention from a practitioner who has matured through three decades of adult self-discovery work.

• conscientious adherence to professional counseling and bodywork ethics.

Steppingstone sessions are an excellent complement to psychotherapy and other healing processes for functional people who are ready to deepen their ability to respond wisely and joyfully to life's challenges.

Q: What professional ethics guide your work?
A: Most important is a clear set of boundaries concerning what offerings are appropriate for Dan's skills and experience. Weekly professional consultations help Dan maintain clarity between personal and client issues; continuing education deepens his sensitivity to hidden inner wounds

and offers abundant methods for healing. Also, you are assured confidentiality in all of our work and can expect personalized referrals when appropriate.

Q: Is it possible to have a *Steppingstone* session that focuses just on inner peace facilitation *or* bodywork, but not both?
A: Yes, of course. You may request this in advance or decide spontaneously after arriving. New clients sometimes prefer only talk in the first session, deciding later if they feel comfortable integrating bodywork also. (Please note, however, that financial arrangements are *per session* and remain the same regardless of that session's activities or length.)

Q: I feel some concern about releasing more blocked-up pain that I can handle. Can we go into these investigations slowly?
A: Certainly! This is why we allow ample time to get to know each other and discover what kinds of processes will be most appropriate for your own unique personal growth experience. You *always* retain control of the situation; when you say stop or ease up, that's what happens.

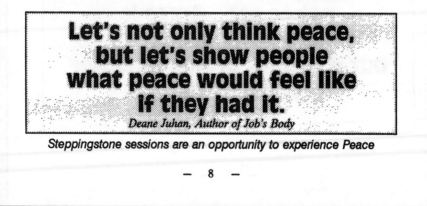

Let's not only think peace, but let's show people what peace would feel like if they had it.
Deane Juhan, Author of Job's Body

Steppingstone sessions are an opportunity to experience Peace

The name *Steppingstone* refers to this experience
as one of many supports on your path
to deeper freedom and wisdom. Each session
is another steppingstone across the river of limitation,
leading to the shores of peace and joy within.

Planning For Your Session

So that your inner peace may unfold most fully, please arrange your *Steppingstone* session so that your time afterwards is open, allowing yourself the freedom to choose whatever activity feels best to you at that time. Often after a session people wish to take a walk, meditate, rest, or write in their journal. Please consider these hours afterwards as an important part of this renewal experience.

Our time together generally averages three hours. Some sessions may complete themselves sooner, and others may run a bit longer. The duration is determined by the natural flow of our process as it evolves that day, not by arbitrary predetermined limits. If unforeseen time constraints do arise for you, however, please mention them at the beginning of the session and our work will be adjusted accordingly.

After your first session, you may decide to continue our work together. Many find it useful to arrange a series of 3 – 5 additional sessions at intervals appropriate to their personal situation. Others return as the need arises.

Steppingstone is located in a peaceful section of Arlington Heights near the Unicorn Bookstore and the Massachusetts Avenue bus. For client convenience, appointments are available on weekday evenings or weekends; other times may also be arranged if necessary. Directions will be given before your first appointment.

A Steppingstone Session Makes An Extraordinary Gift
Beautiful Gift Certificates Are Available

**Professional ethical standards for bodywork and counseling
are fully adhered to in all Steppingstone sessions
Confidentiality Guaranteed**

Financial Information

*Steppingstone offers
three payment options*

• *The standard fee for a Steppingstone session is $95.* This amount attempts to balance the intensive length of time we work together with a very modest hourly rate for experienced professional counseling and bodywork.*

• *If the standard price for this work is not appropriate for your current financial situation,* a sliding scale of $55 to $95 is also offered. The honor system is used; you decide what amount is appropriate for you at the completion of your first session.

• *If you feel sincerely drawn to what Steppingstone offers,* but even an amount in the sliding scale range is beyond your means, *please do come and whatever you offer for the first session will be joyfully accepted.*

> **As a healing arts professional, it is my commitment
> that these services be financially accessible
> to any client who is sincerely drawn to this work
> and is ready to incorporate what is offered
> in their personal and spiritual development.**

If you choose to continue
the work we begin together in our first session,
we will arrange an ongoing session fee that is appropriate
for you based upon your current financial situation and the
frequency of your sessions. You are, of course, free to discuss
and renegotiate financial arrangements at any time.

Thank you for the integrity you bring to this process

*One way to think about the fee is that a *Steppingstone* session is the equivalent of 1 – 1½ hours of counseling *plus* a 1 – 1½ hour massage/bodywork session, *each costing $50 – $80 by themselves.* However, the total fee for these *Steppingstone* sessions has purposely been kept low to allow participation by people from various economic levels.

The Vision

This is a call to you who are in the process of transforming your life and evolving beyond the tension and limitations which others consider normal. It is an invitation to use Steppingstone's unique combination of insightful counseling and transformation oriented bodywork to support your growth as a spiritual warrior - a person increasingly focused on becoming empowered in the service of your highest vision, the healing of our human family and our wounded Mother Earth.

This invitation is especially for you who are committed to personal, social, organizational, and planetary transformation, and who may currently be feeling the need for additional support in maintaining your inner peace and clarity of purpose.

The Experience Awaits You

Dan Menkin, Steppingstone
Arlington Heights, MA
(800) 442-6035

Steppingstone Is Committed To Financial Accessibility
(See page 14 for details)

Printed on recycled paper - please recycle by sharing with a friend

About the Author

Dan Menkin, operating as Steppingstone Massage, has facilitated thousands of three-hour sessions since 1984 integrating spiritual and personal counseling with transformation-oriented bodywork. In 1968, after having received a bachelor's degree in sociology and having spent several years in business administration, Dan began his massage training with a workshop at the Esalen Institute. In the early 1970s he organized and lead numerous massage retreat workshops and other personal-growth trainings. During this time he cofounded The Humanistic Massage Guild of Greater Boston, an organization of professionals devoted to high ethical standards and public education.

In 1975 Dan left his "worldly" life to pursue a spiritual quest focusing on meditation and introspection. Five years later he returned to "normal life" feeling humbled and not knowing how to proceed. Living in Santa Rosa, California, he spent the early 1980s surviving and serving others through work as a handyman, a houseparent in a home for developmentally disabled adolescents, an aide for disabled seniors, and a volunteer coordinator for an Adopt-A-Grandparent program. During this time he also experienced three years of parenthood as an "adopted" father to a fatherless boy.

As he turned forty in 1984, Dan returned to the Boston area, began his combined bodywork and counseling practice, and became involved with men's consciousness raising, founding local professional bodywork associations, and studying personal, spiritual, and planetary evolution. He is cofounder of the Transformation-Oriented Bodywork Network (TOB-Net) and founder of the Guild of (financially) Accessible Practitioners (see resources in chapter 21).

The late 1980s opened a new phase in Dan's life, as he began writing more and seeing his work published in a variety of periodicals. Included were many of his spiritual short stories as well as a variety of articles on personal and planetary transformation, healing, the process of spiritual awakening, and the psychological aspects of bodywork. Since November 1993, *Massage* magazine has been publishing his regular column entitled "Facilitating Inner Peace: Exploring Ways to Support Clients in their Quest for Enduring Relaxation."

Dan's first self-published book, 'Upon a Time Tales, is a collection of fourteen fantasies written to "massage" the mind, loosen old, tight habits of perception, and hint at the freedom to be found on the other side of "What if . . . ?" These spiritual stories deal with subjects such as a computer "dating" service where adventures with an ideal mate are computer-projected directly into the "client's" nervous system, a painfully shy lad who discovers a pair of x-ray glasses that allow him to see into other people's hearts, a little girl whose father's movie theater shows movies right out of her mind, and a magnetic world where metallic people are constantly attracting or repelling each other. (Copies can be ordered from the author using the phone number listed below.)

Dan's "Facilitating Inner Peace" workshops are offered in various locations around the country. They include private four-hour sessions for each participant plus a day of group work and provide ten CEUs for NCTMB recertification. These workshops allow healing arts professionals to experience personally the processes described in Transformation Through Bodywork. Participants are encouraged to form ongoing peer support groups for enhancing and deepening their insights and skills. Support for organizing a local chapter of the Guild of (financially) Accessible Practitioners is also available, if desired. For additional information, call (800) 442-6035.